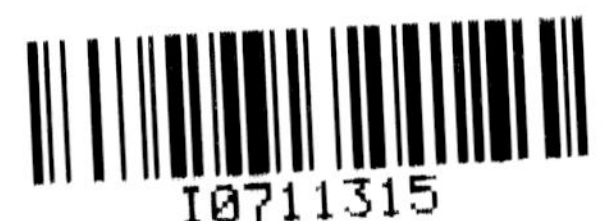

Sugar Skulls

Day Of The Dead

Coloring Book For Adults

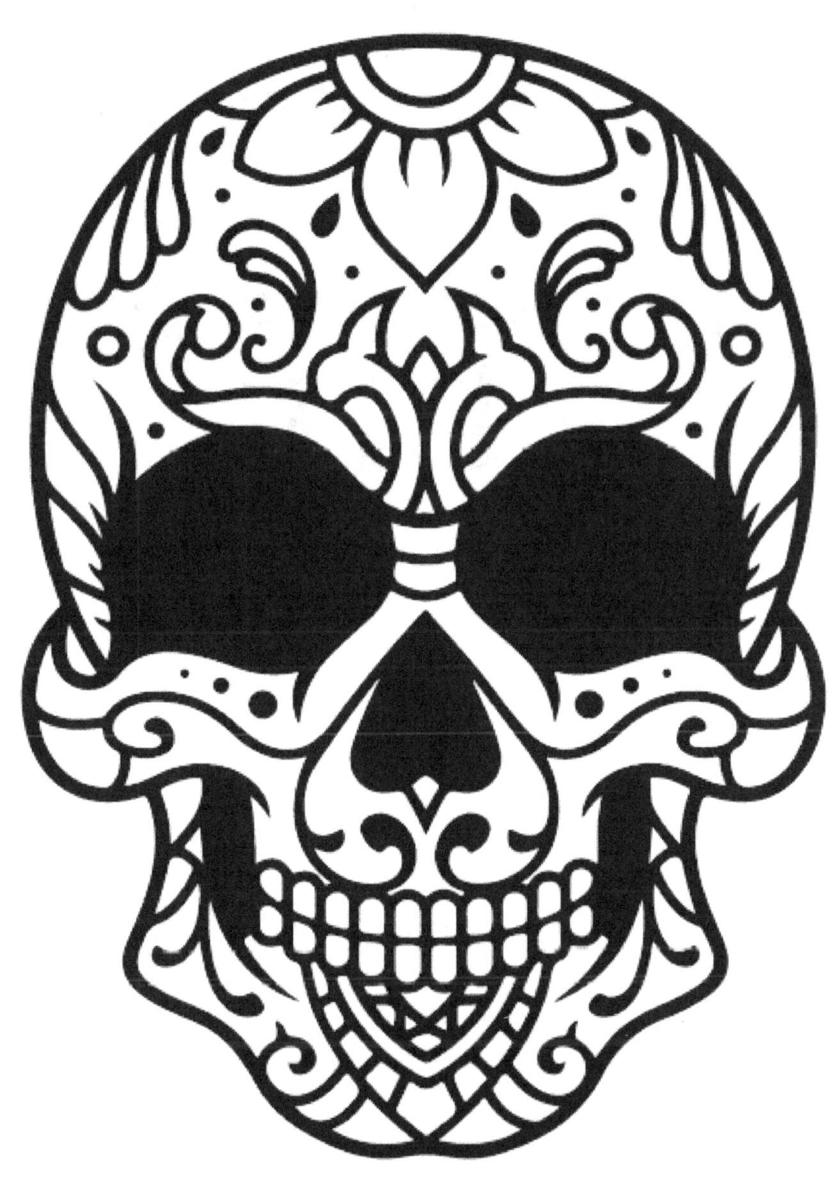

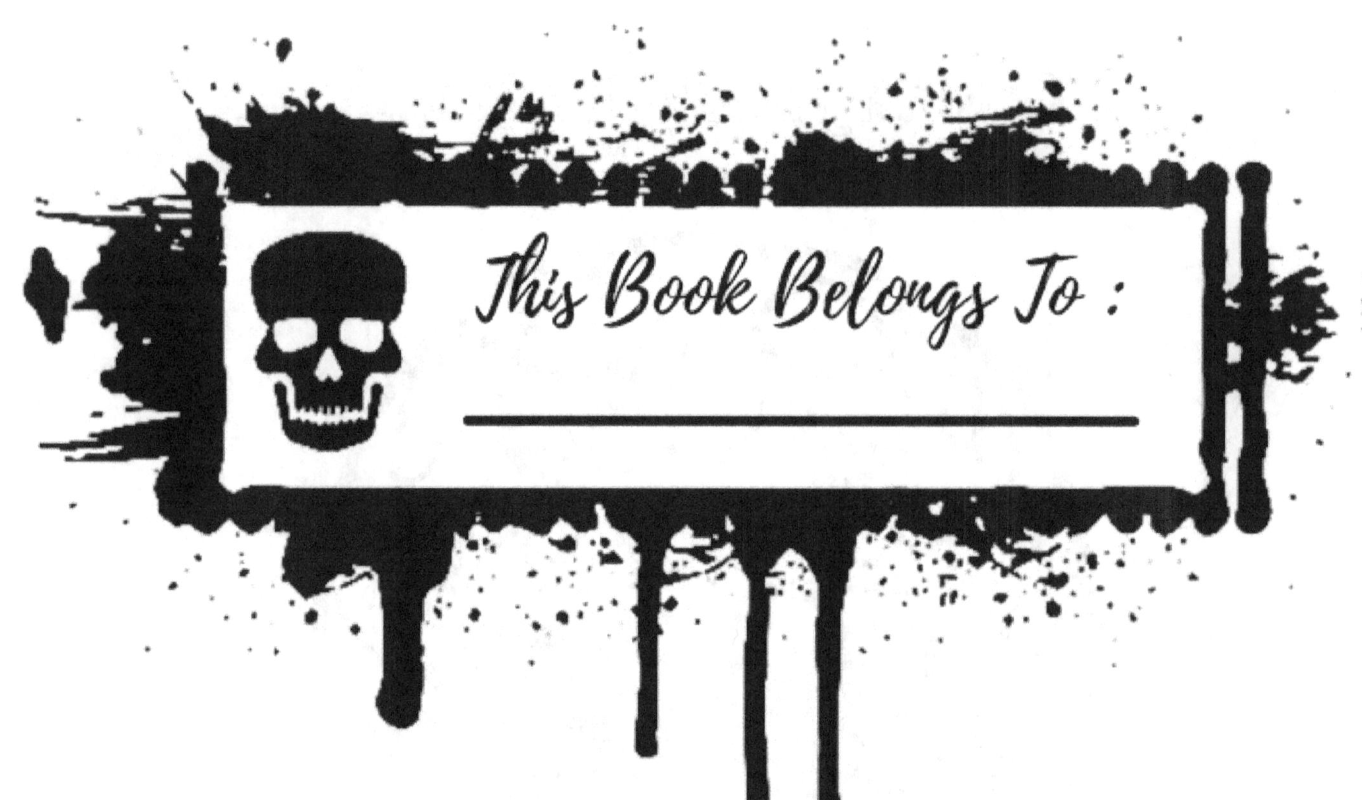
This Book Belongs To :

Color Test

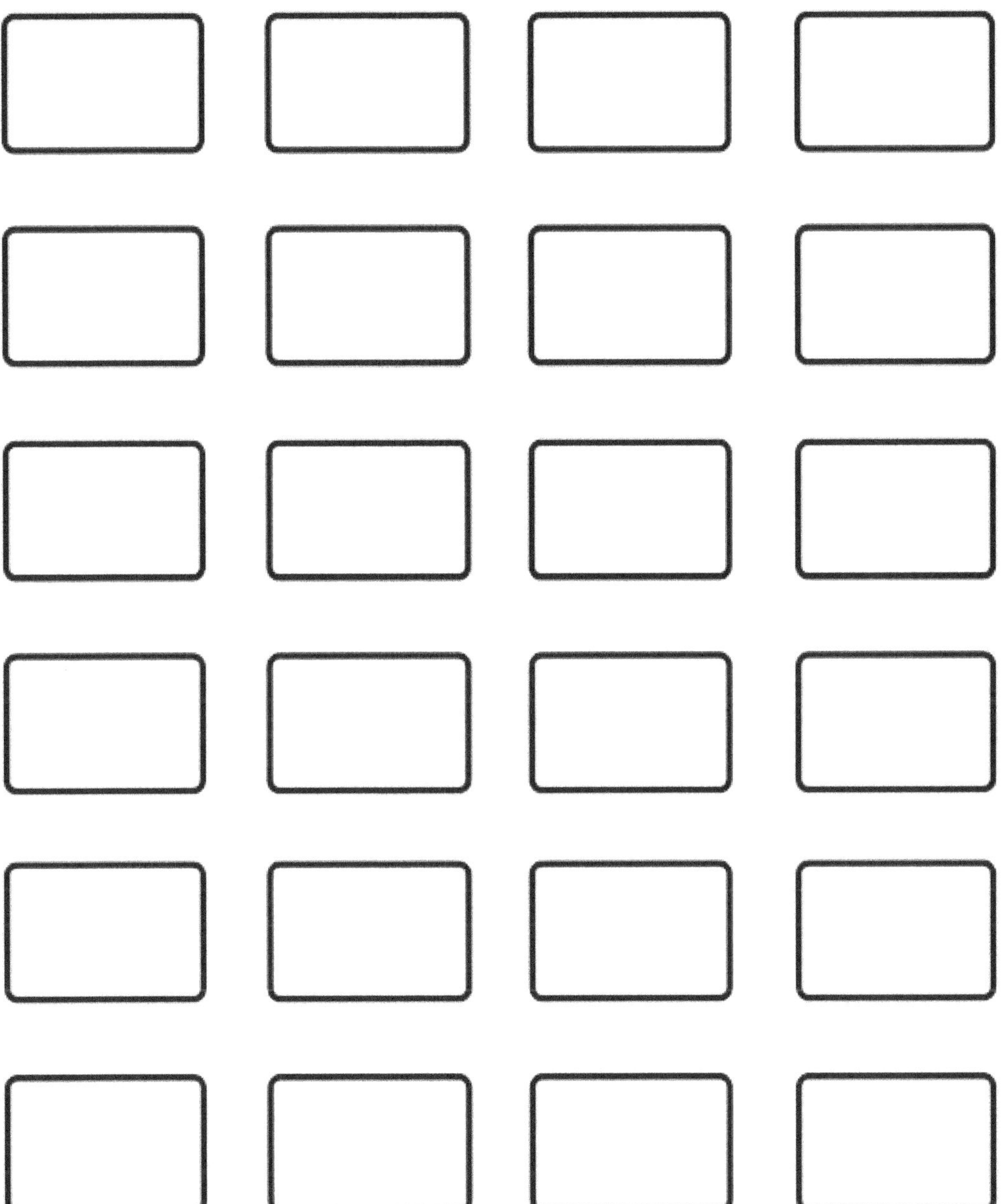

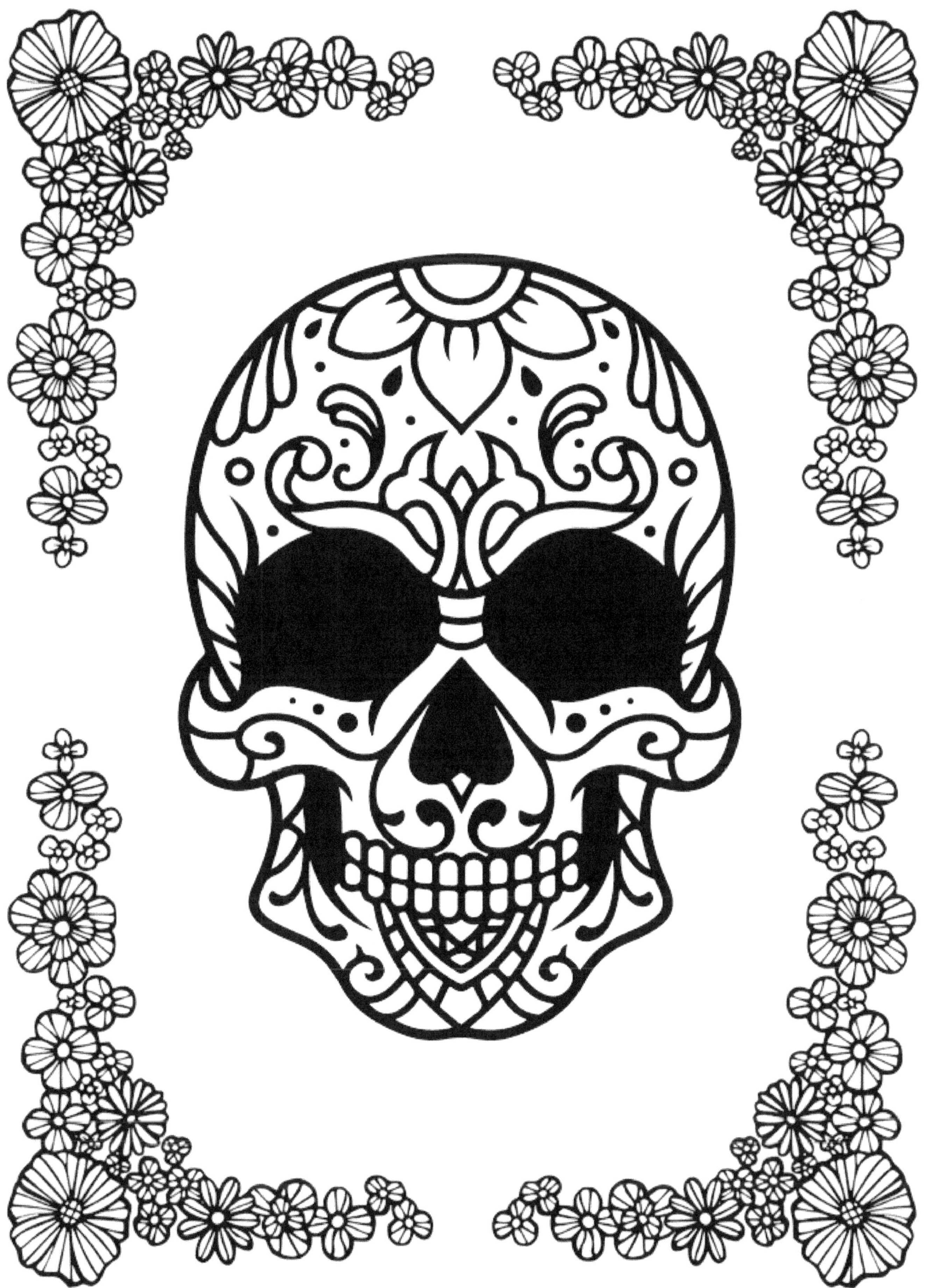

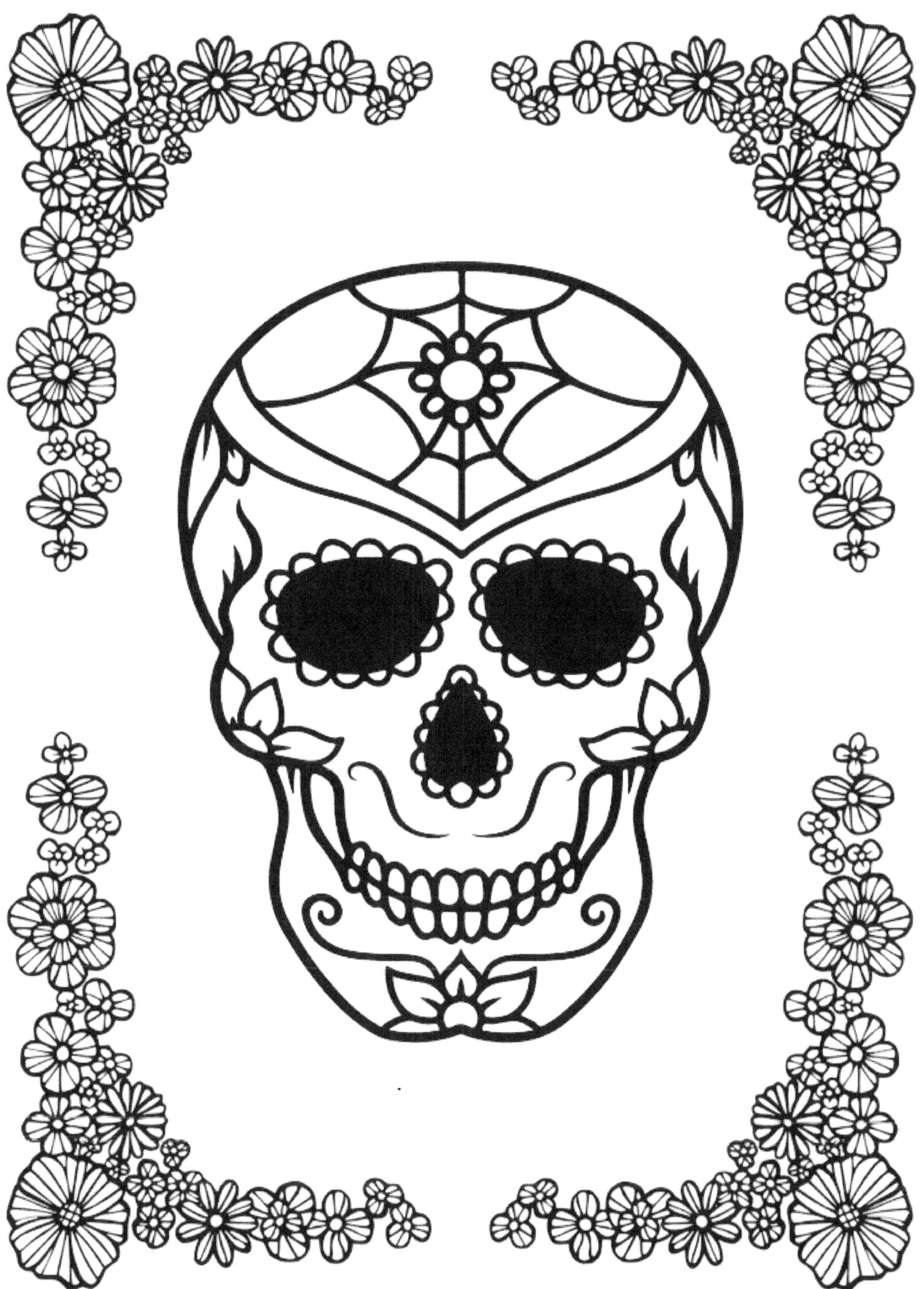

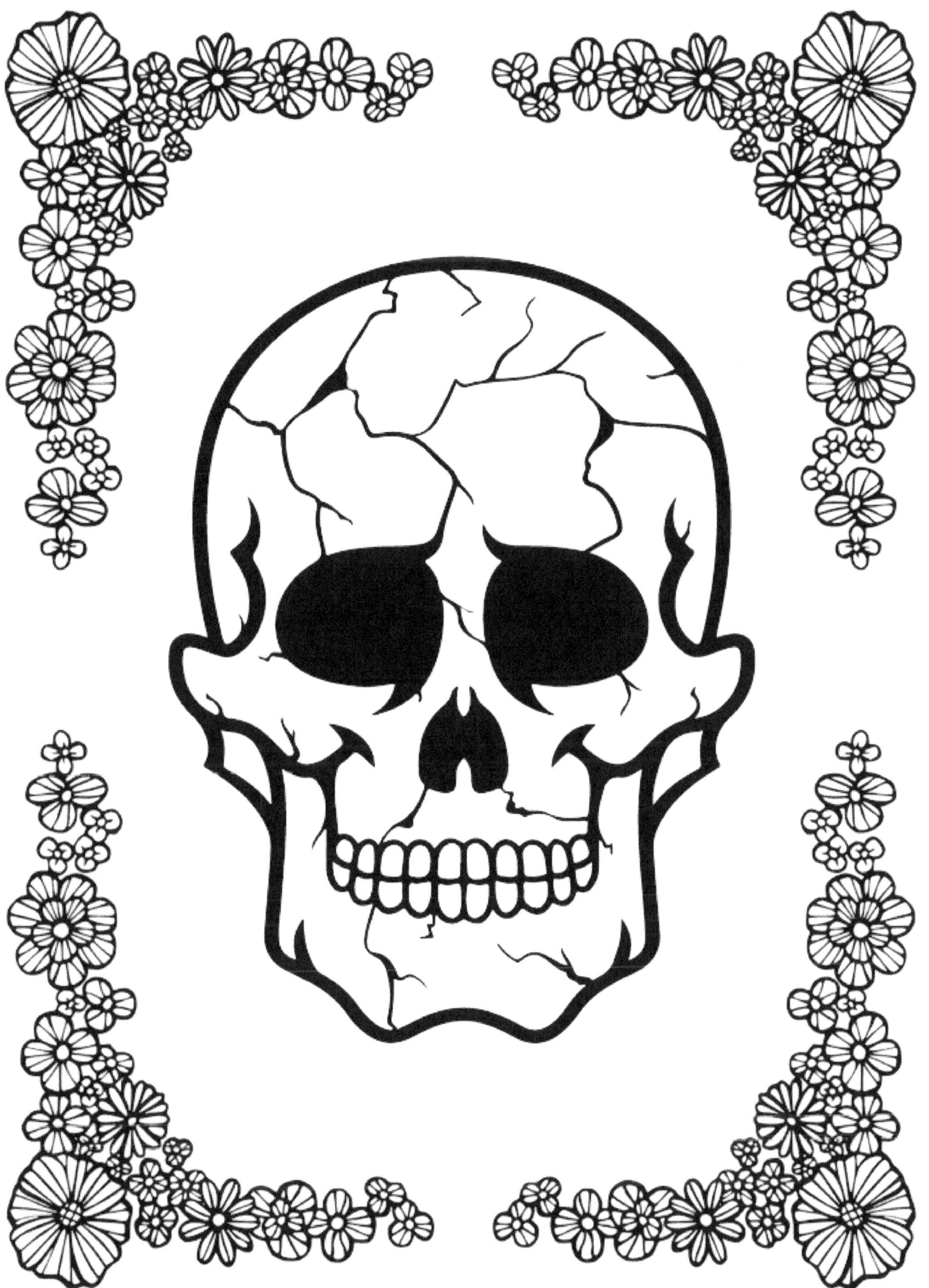

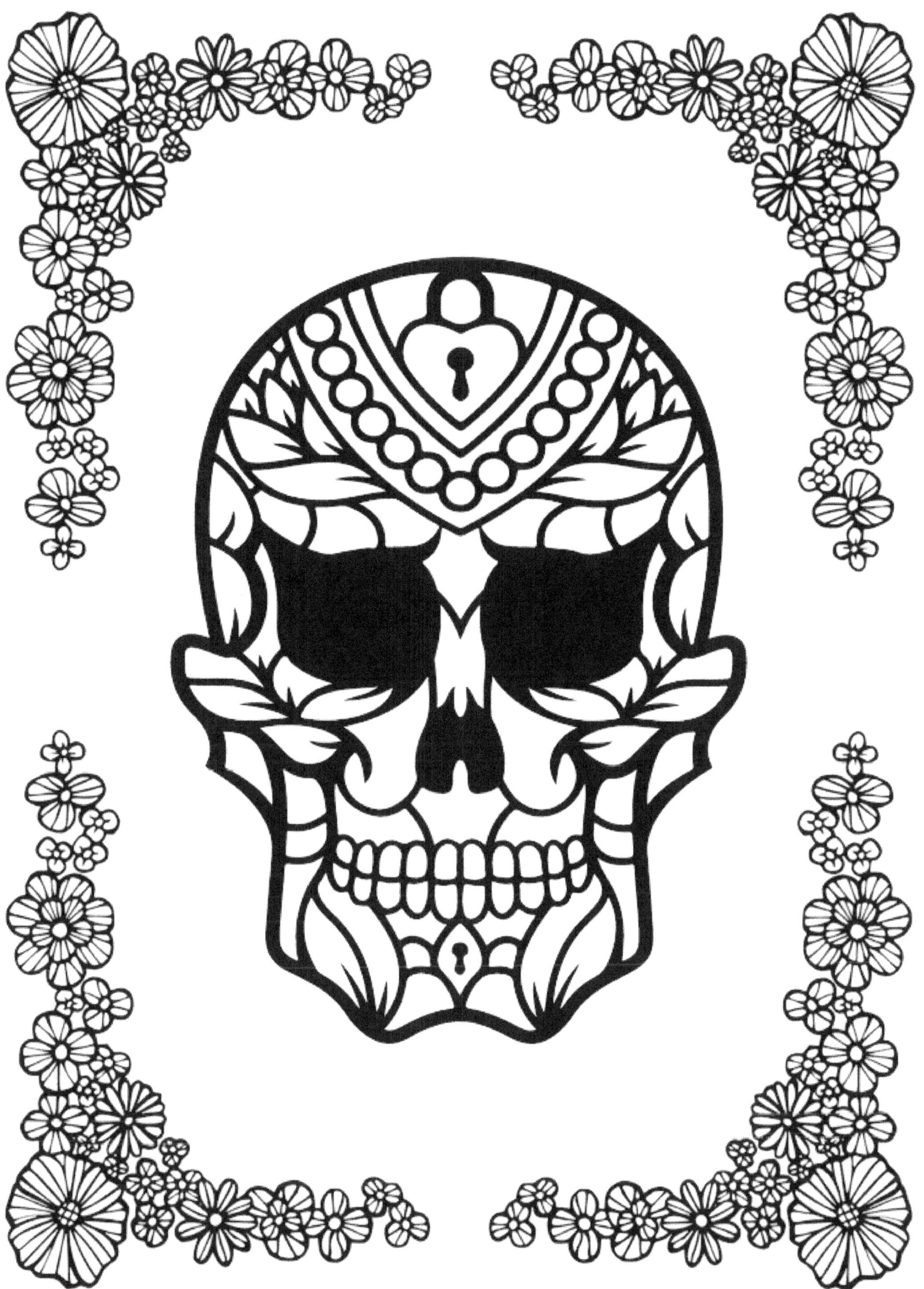

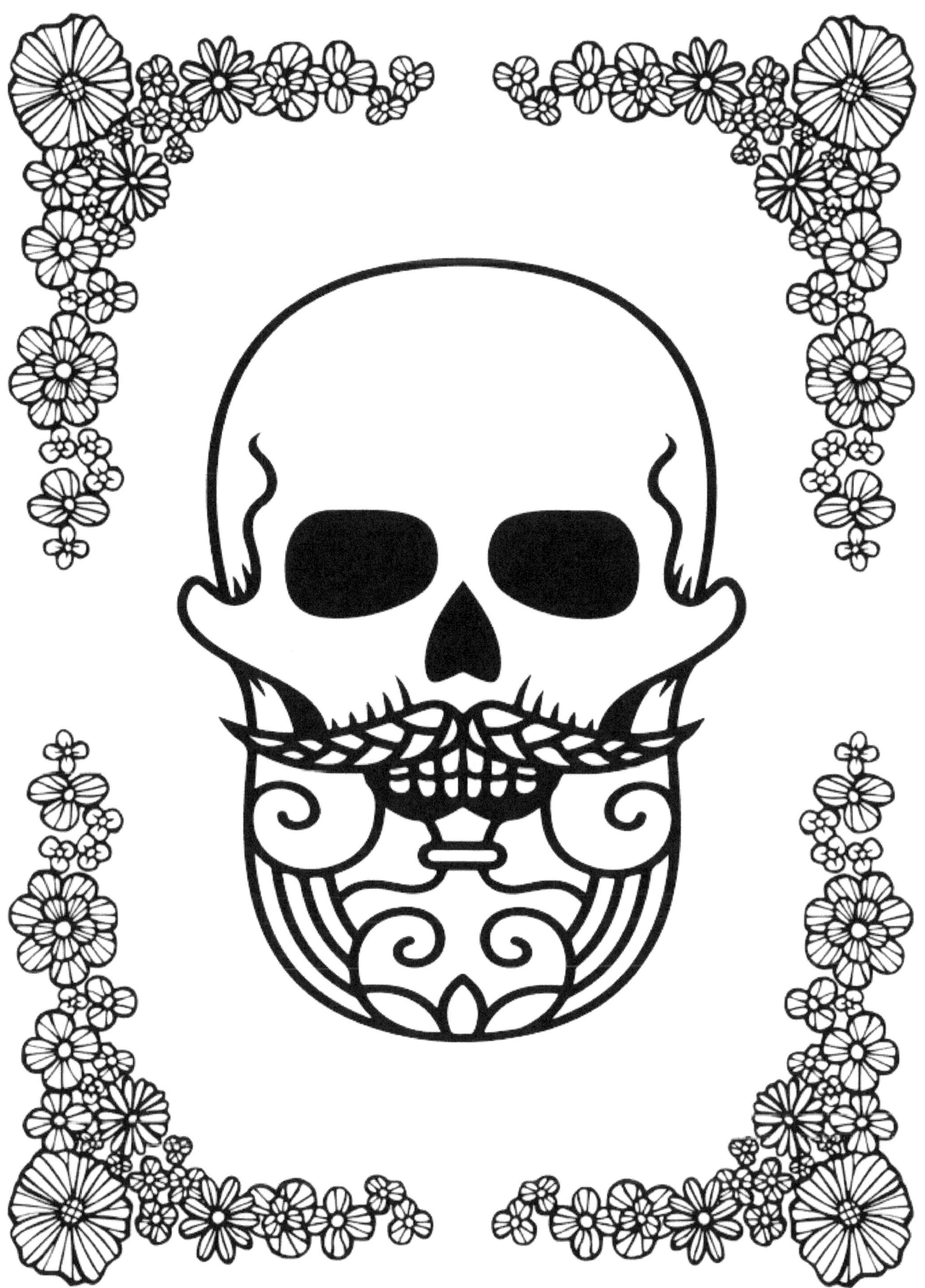

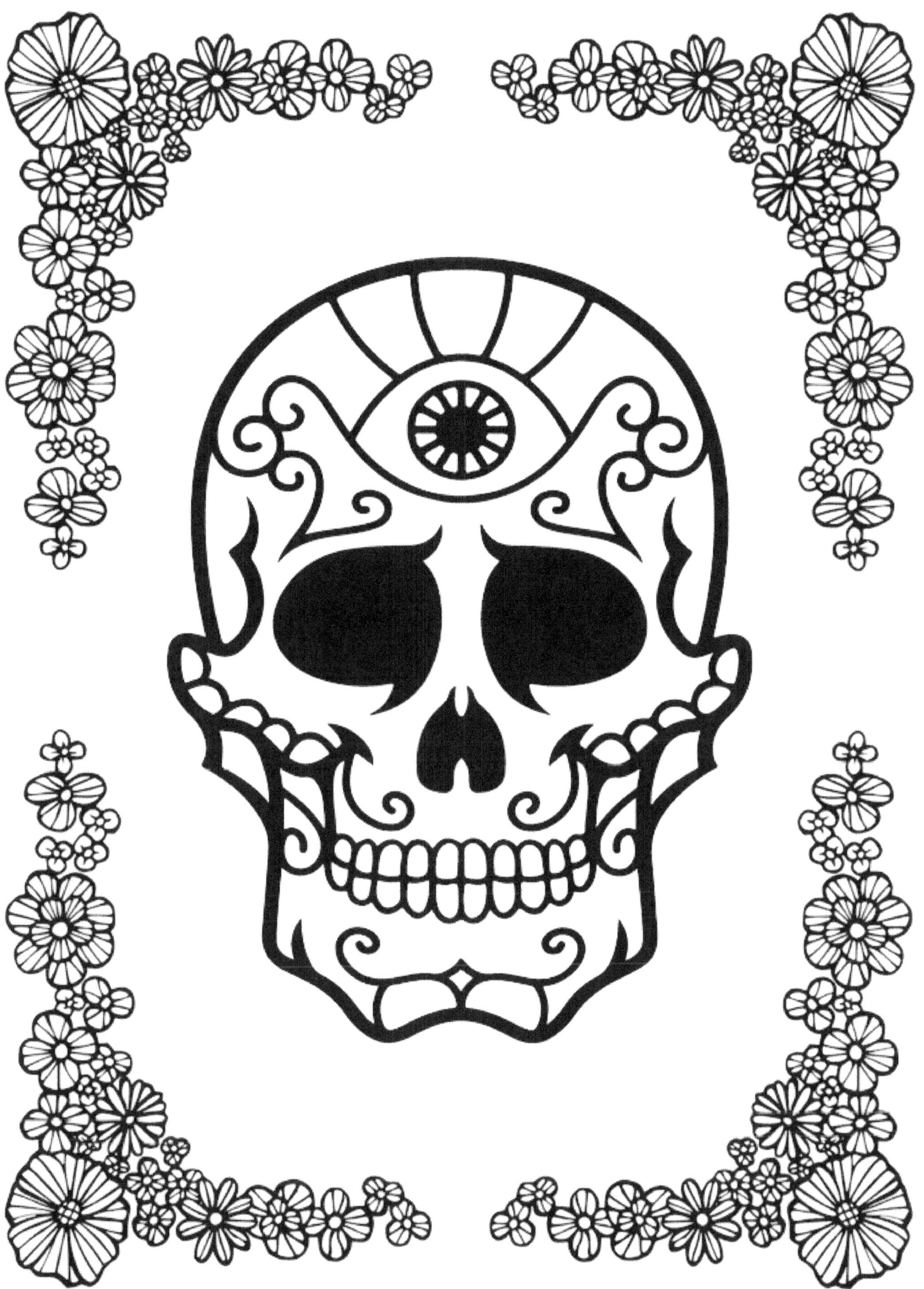

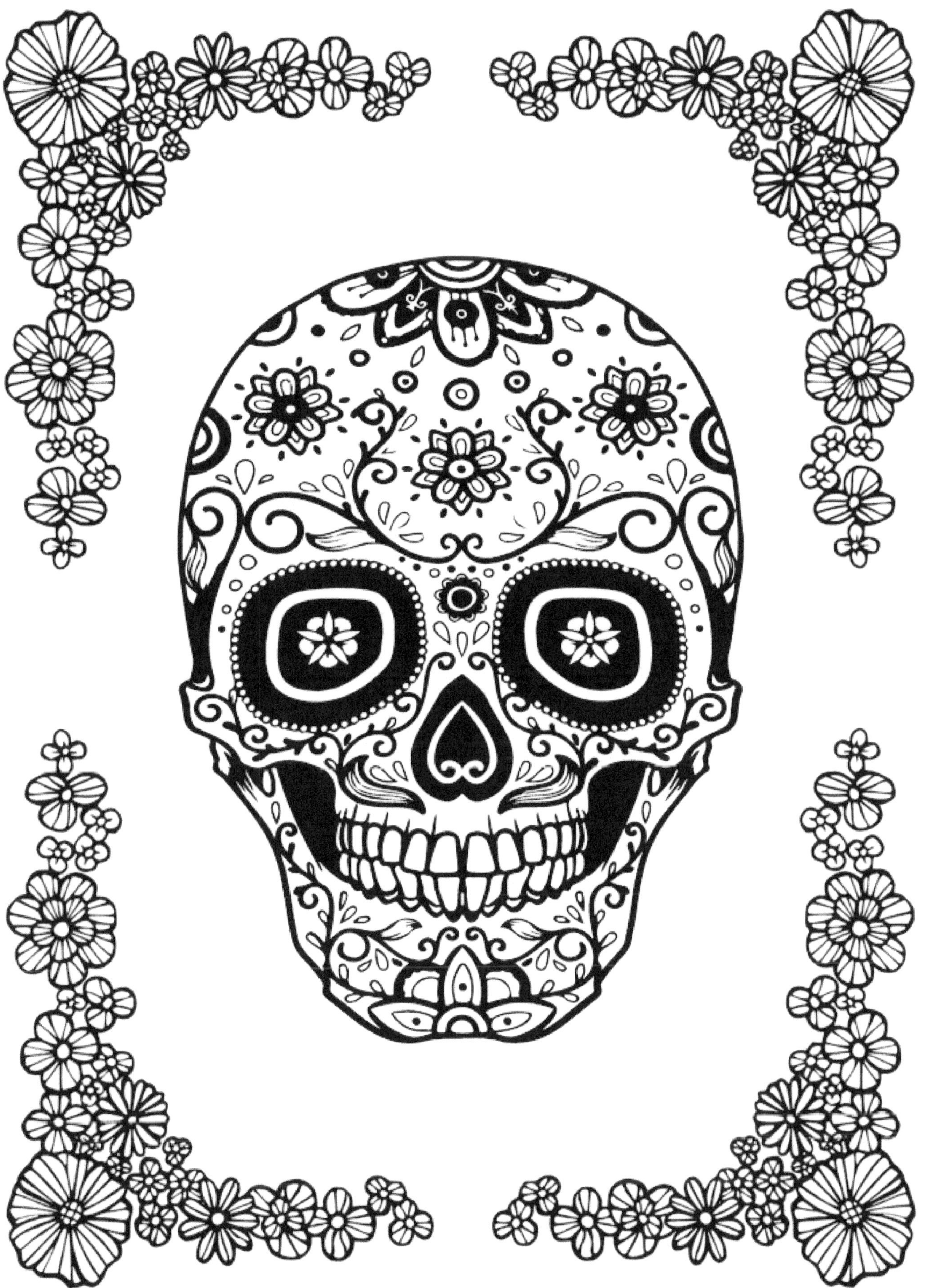

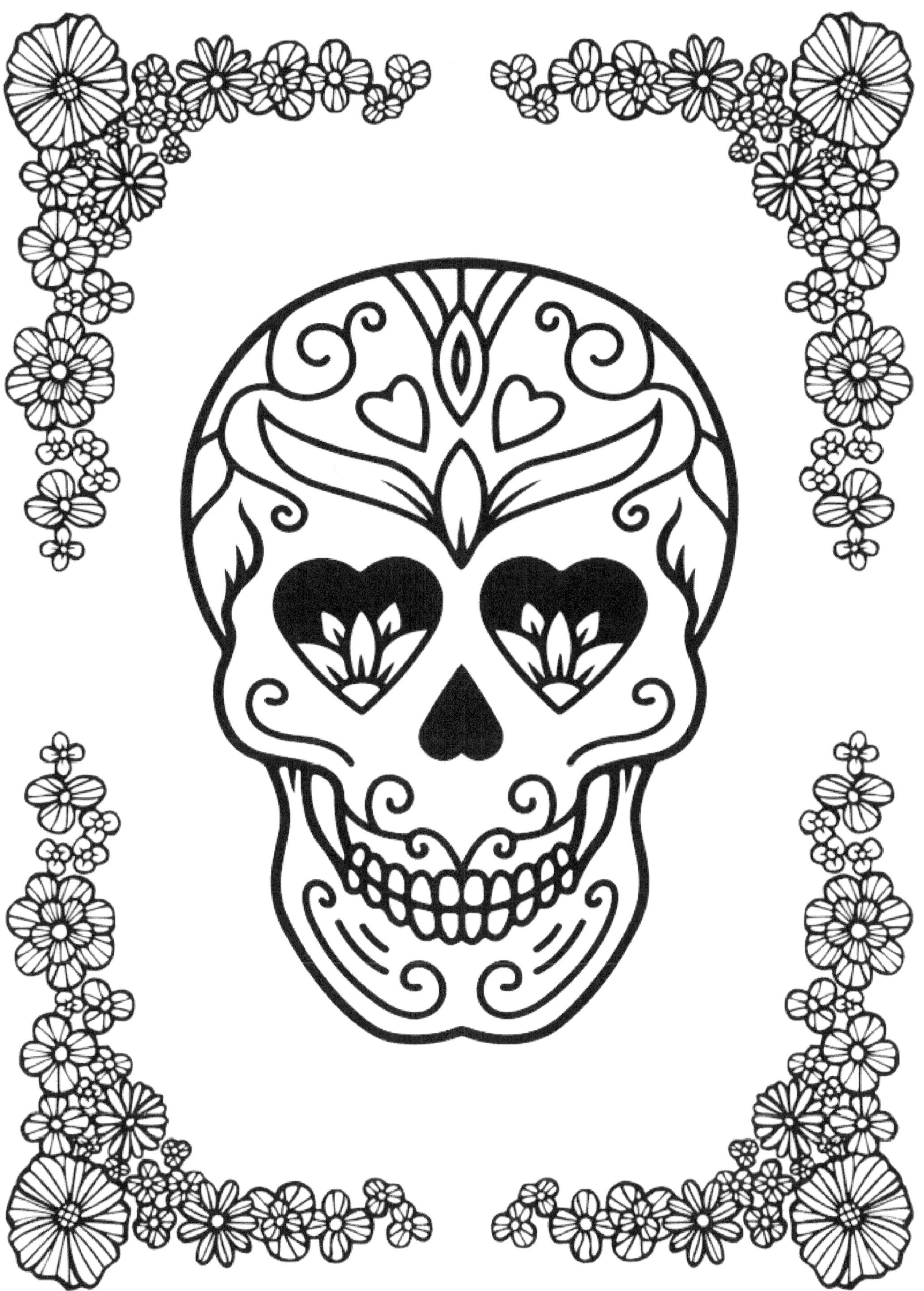

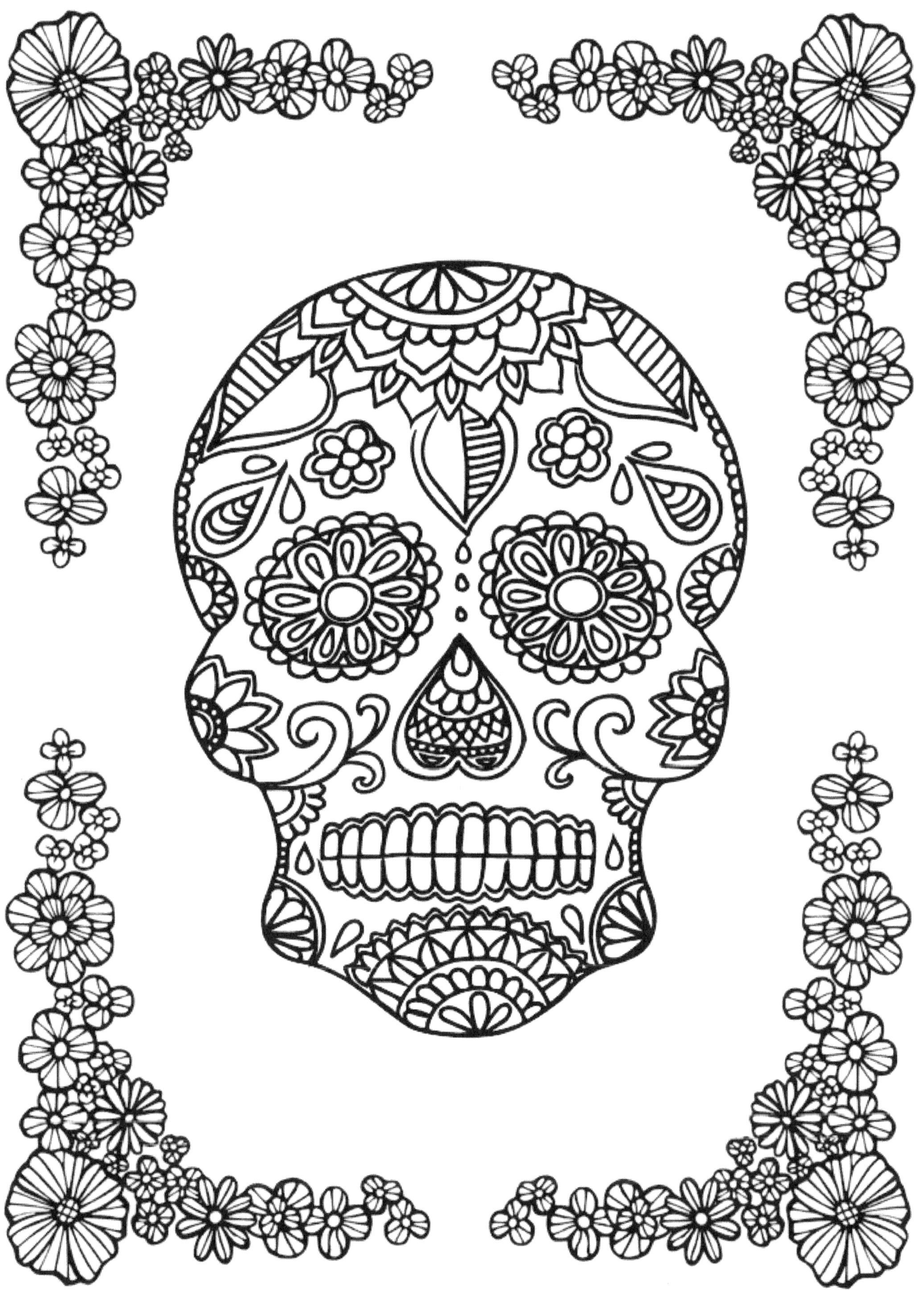

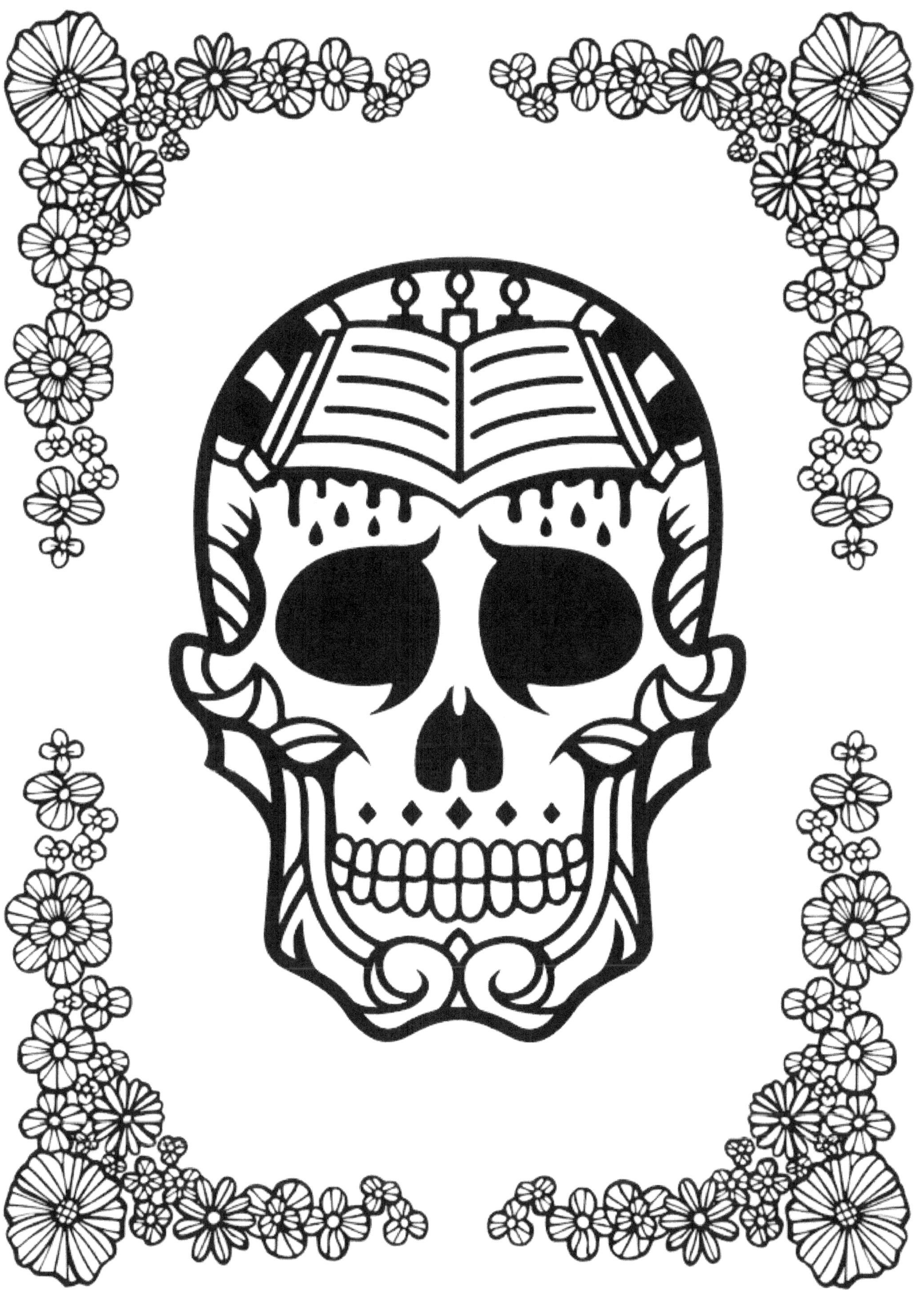

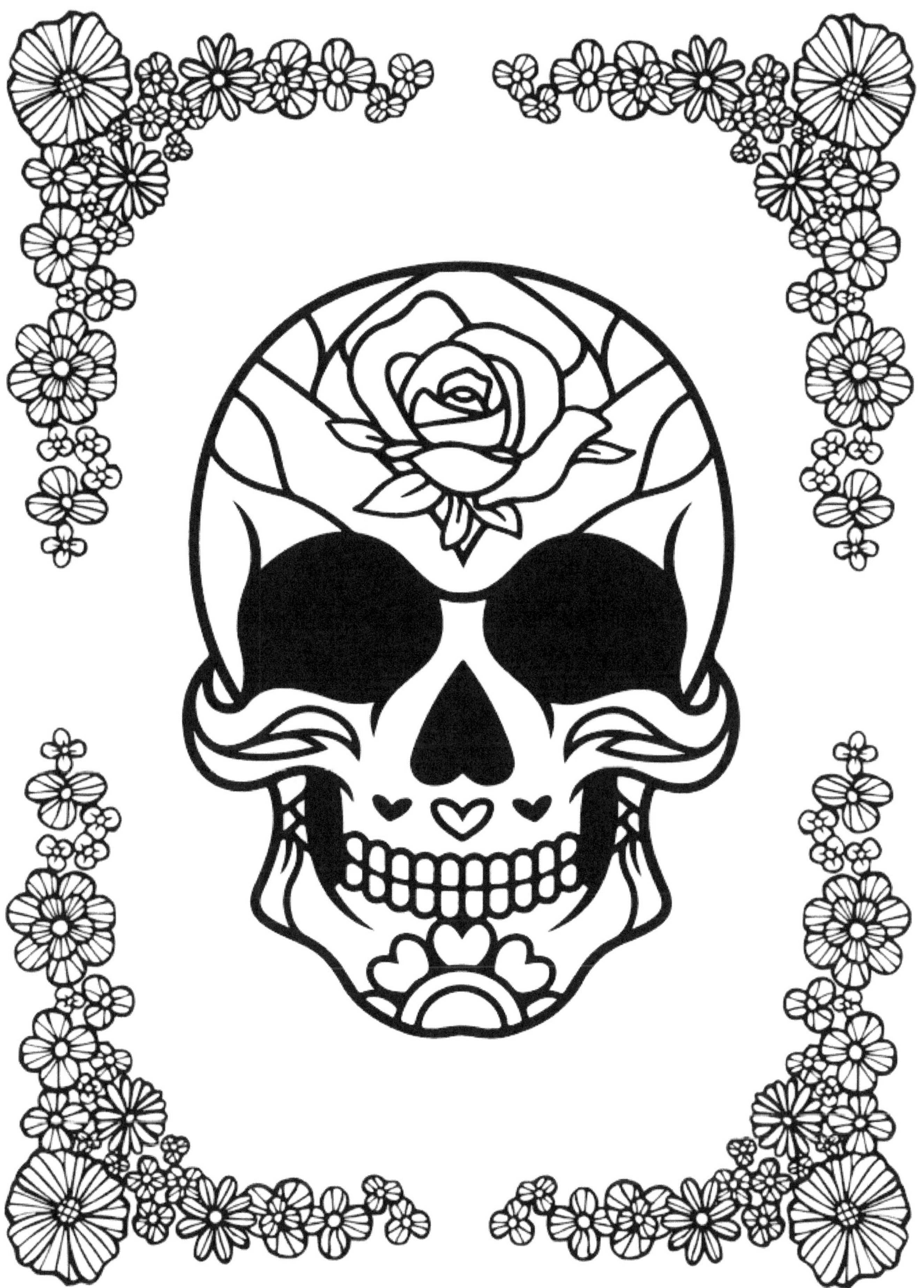

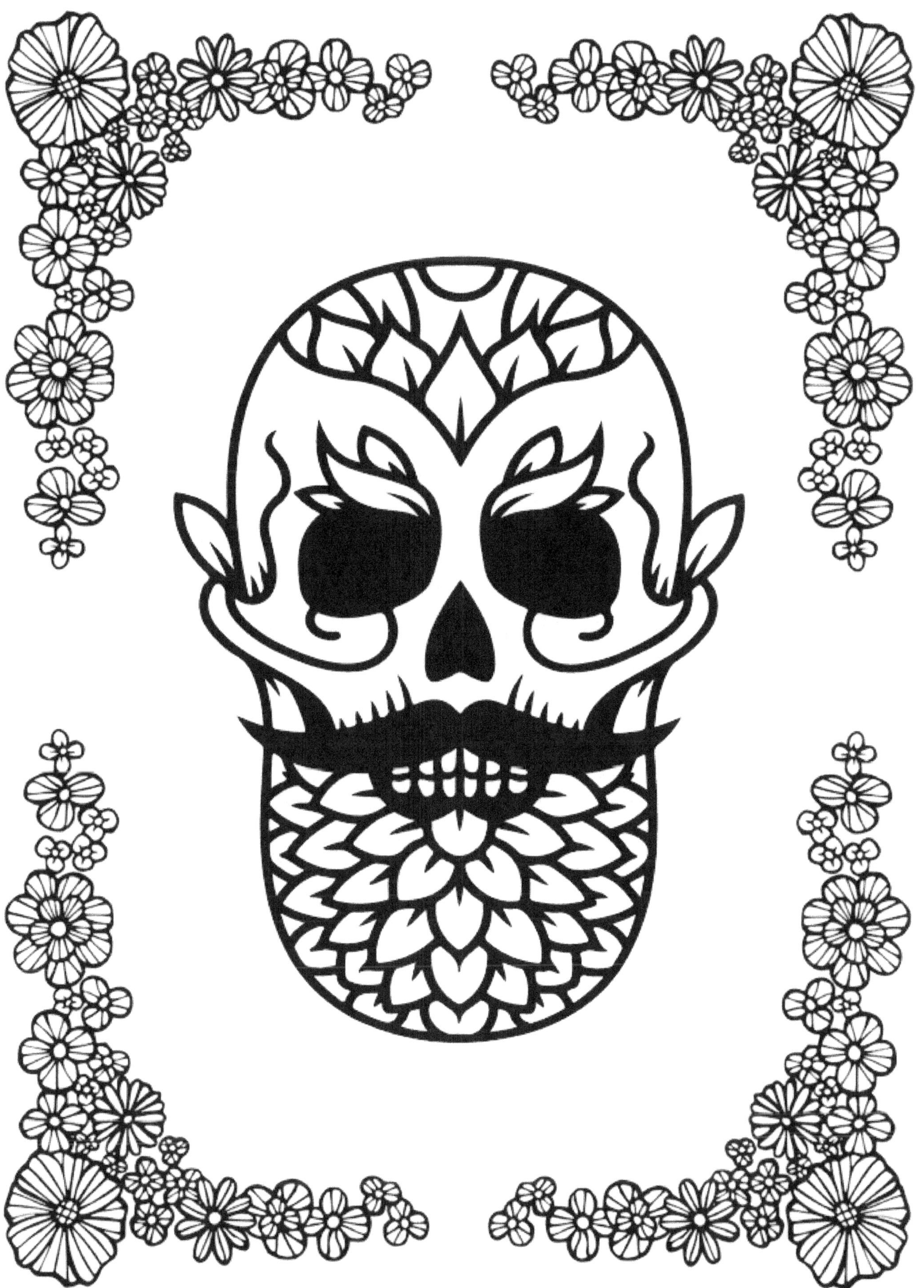

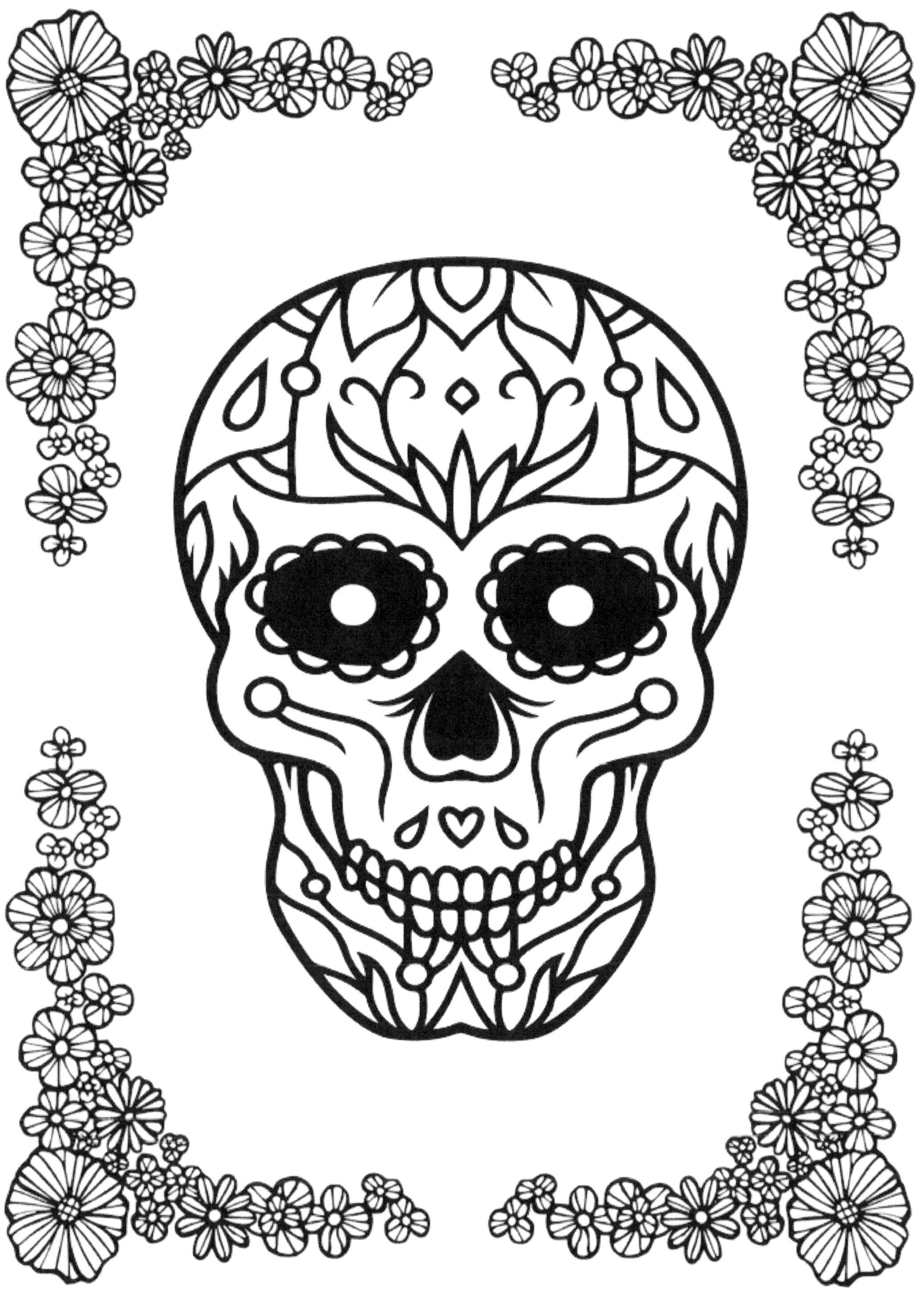

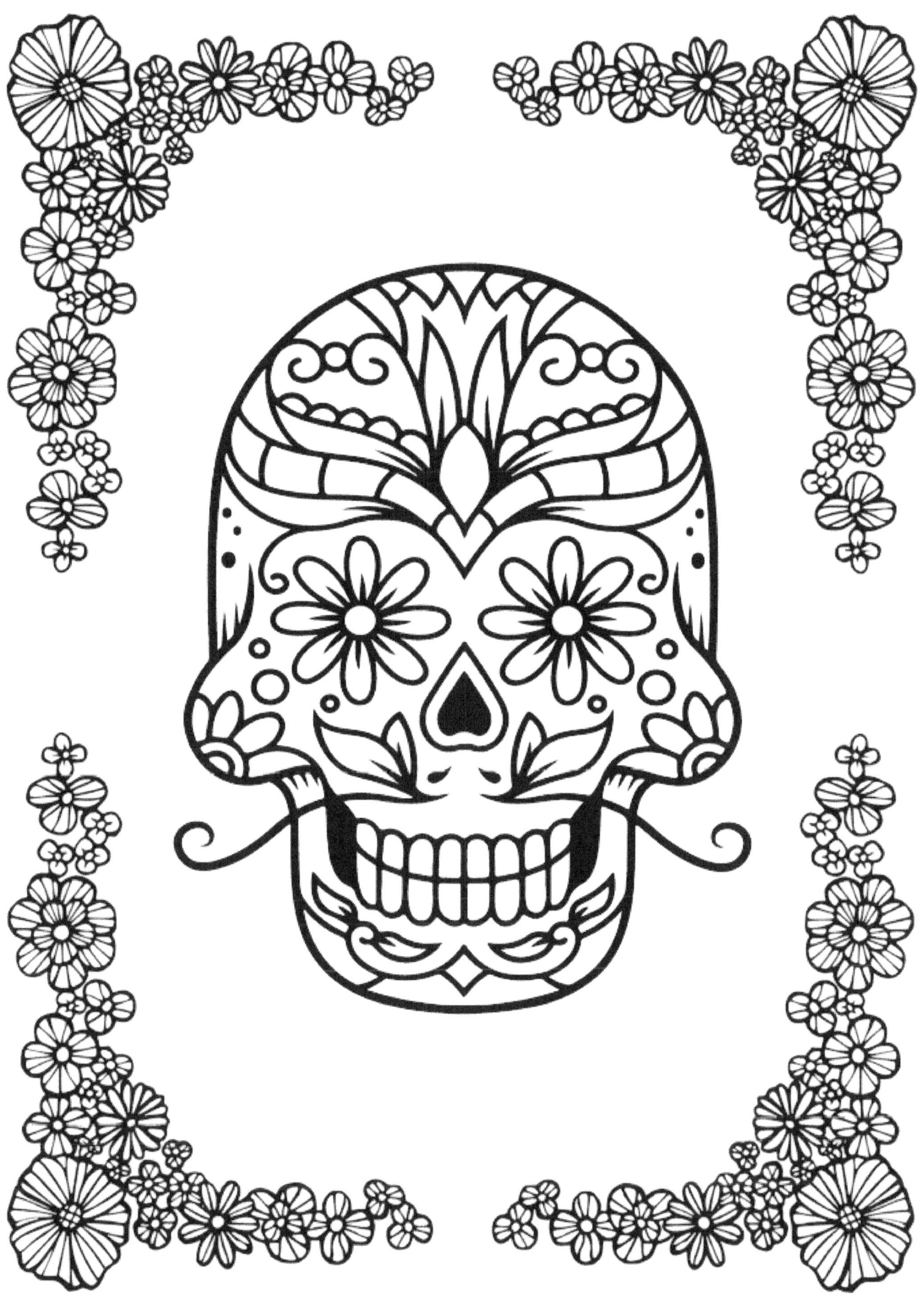

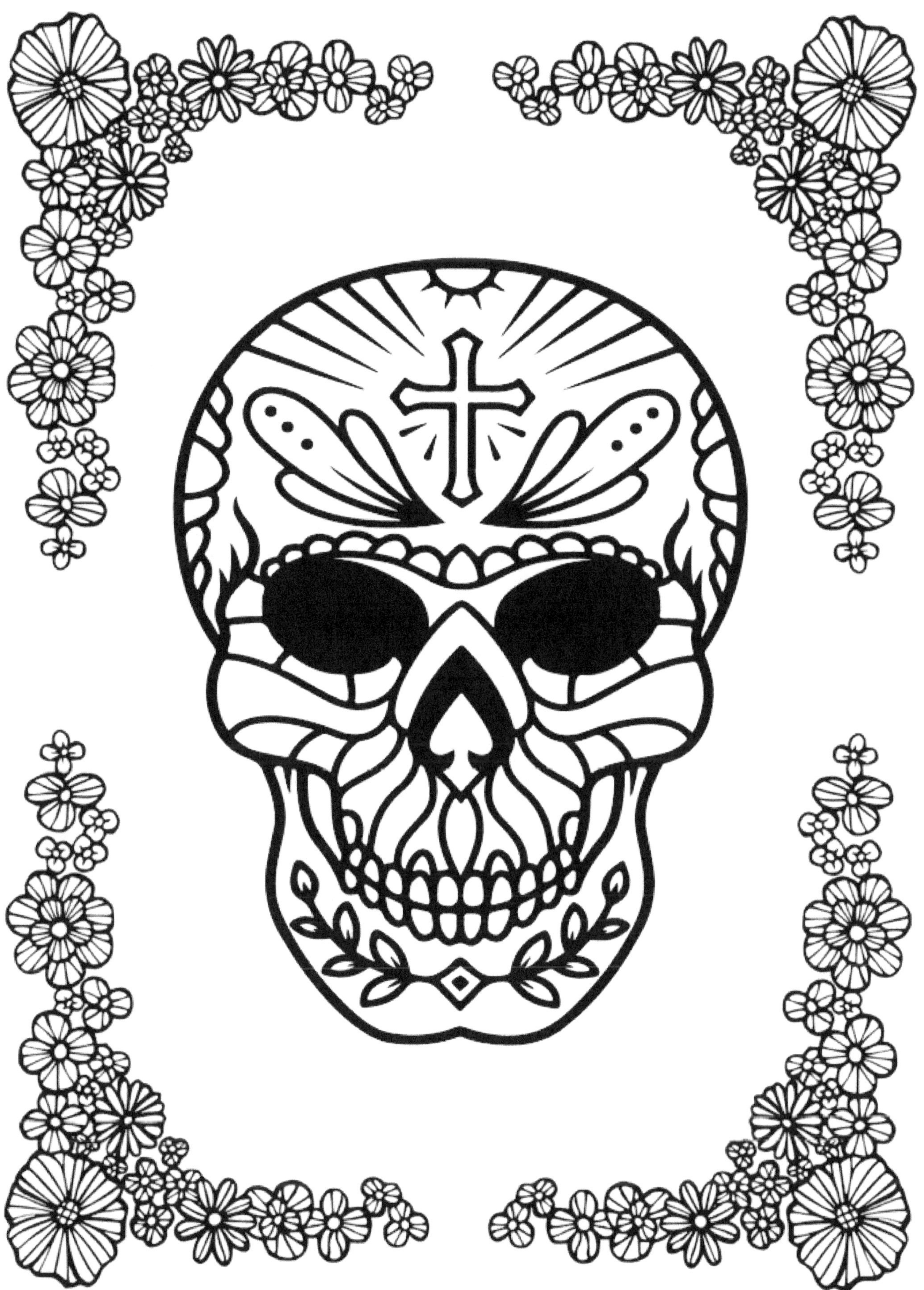

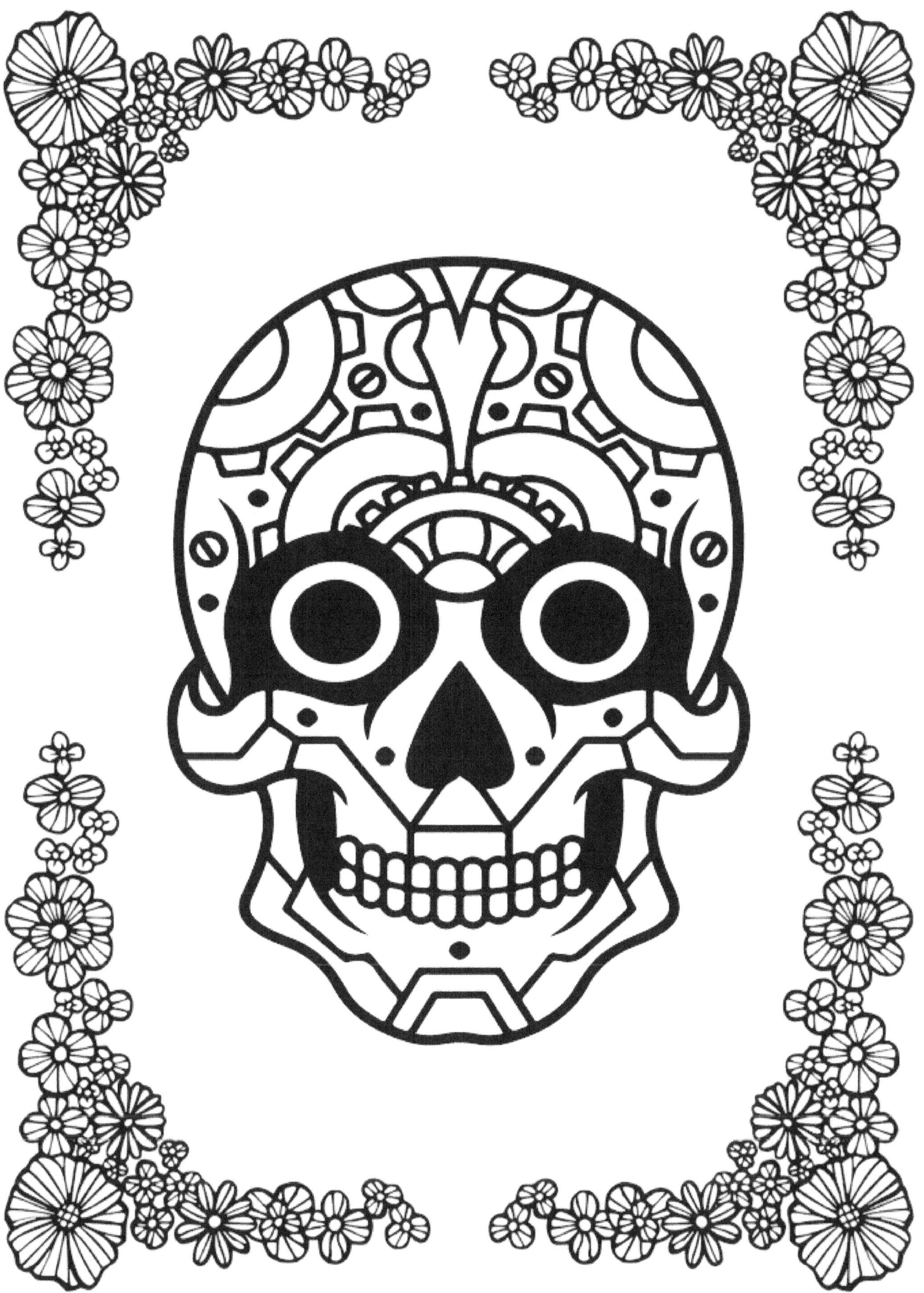

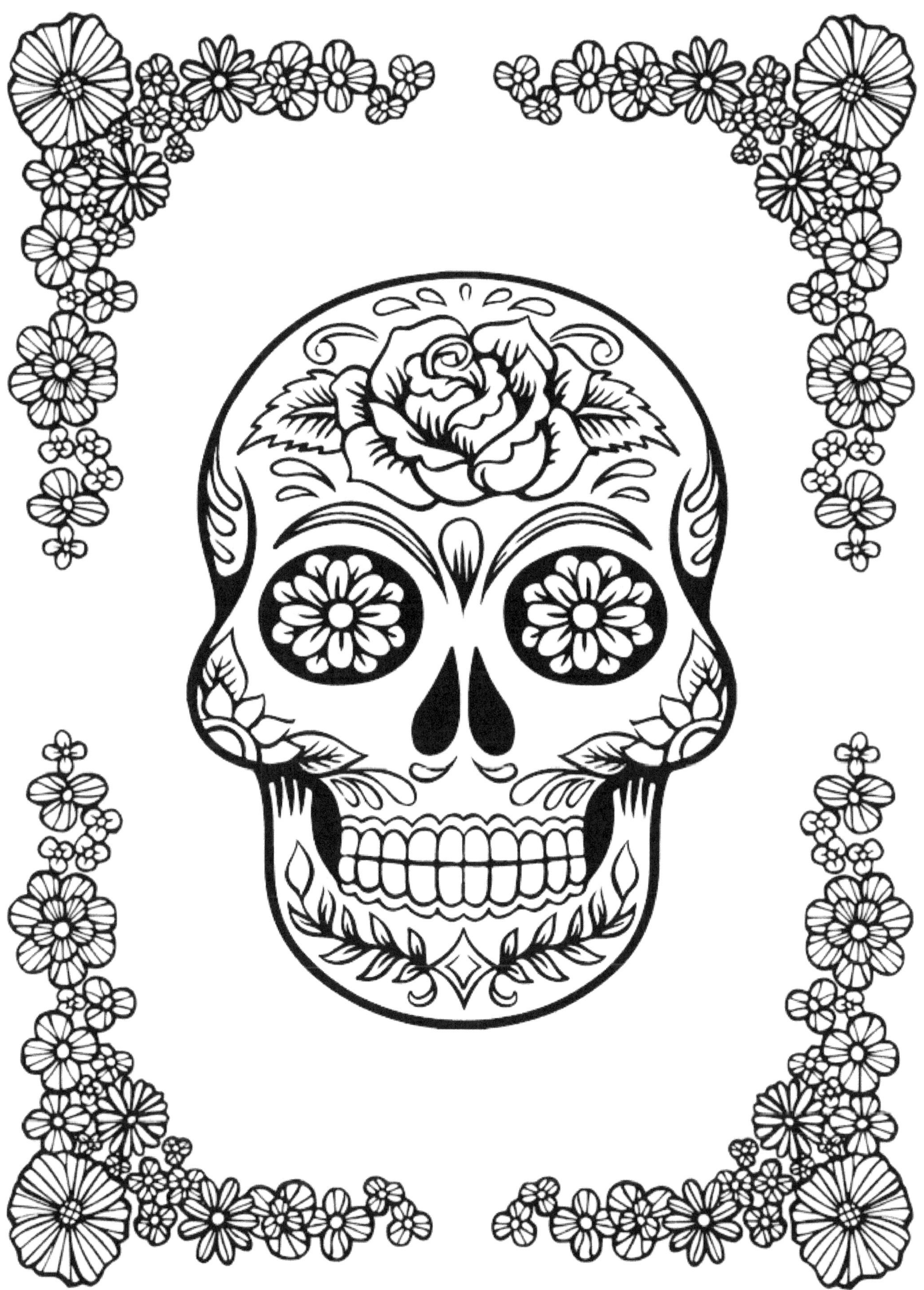

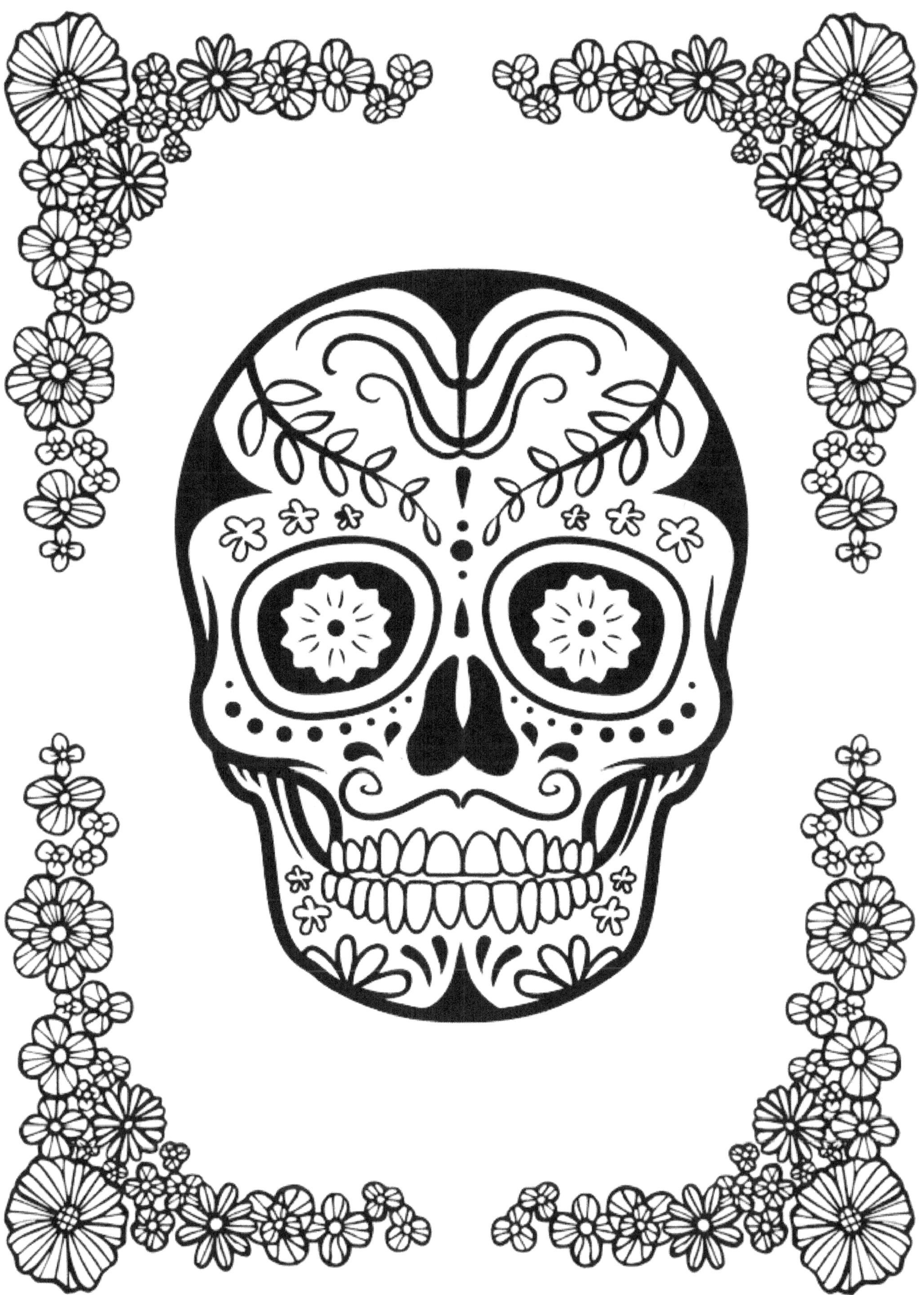

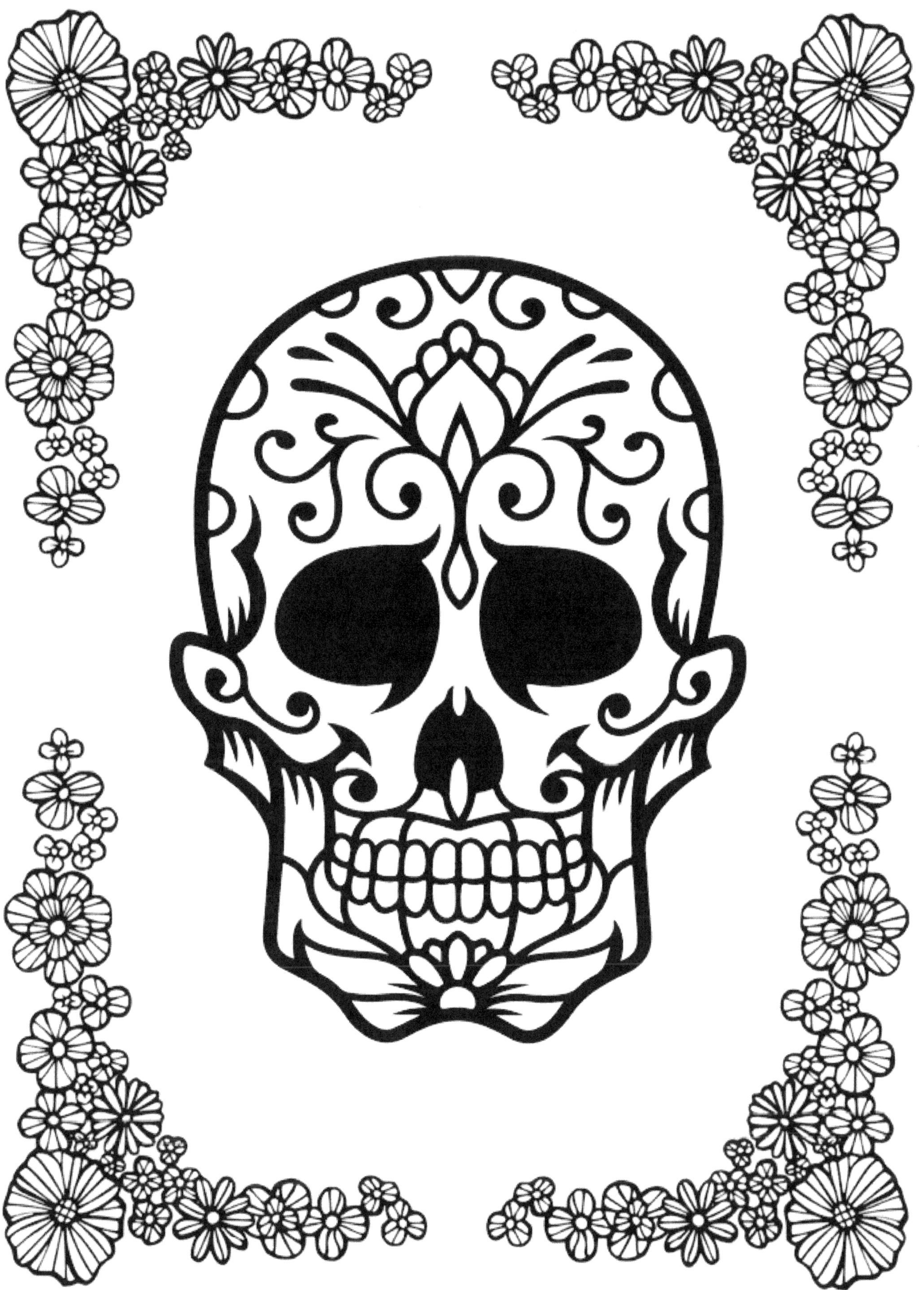

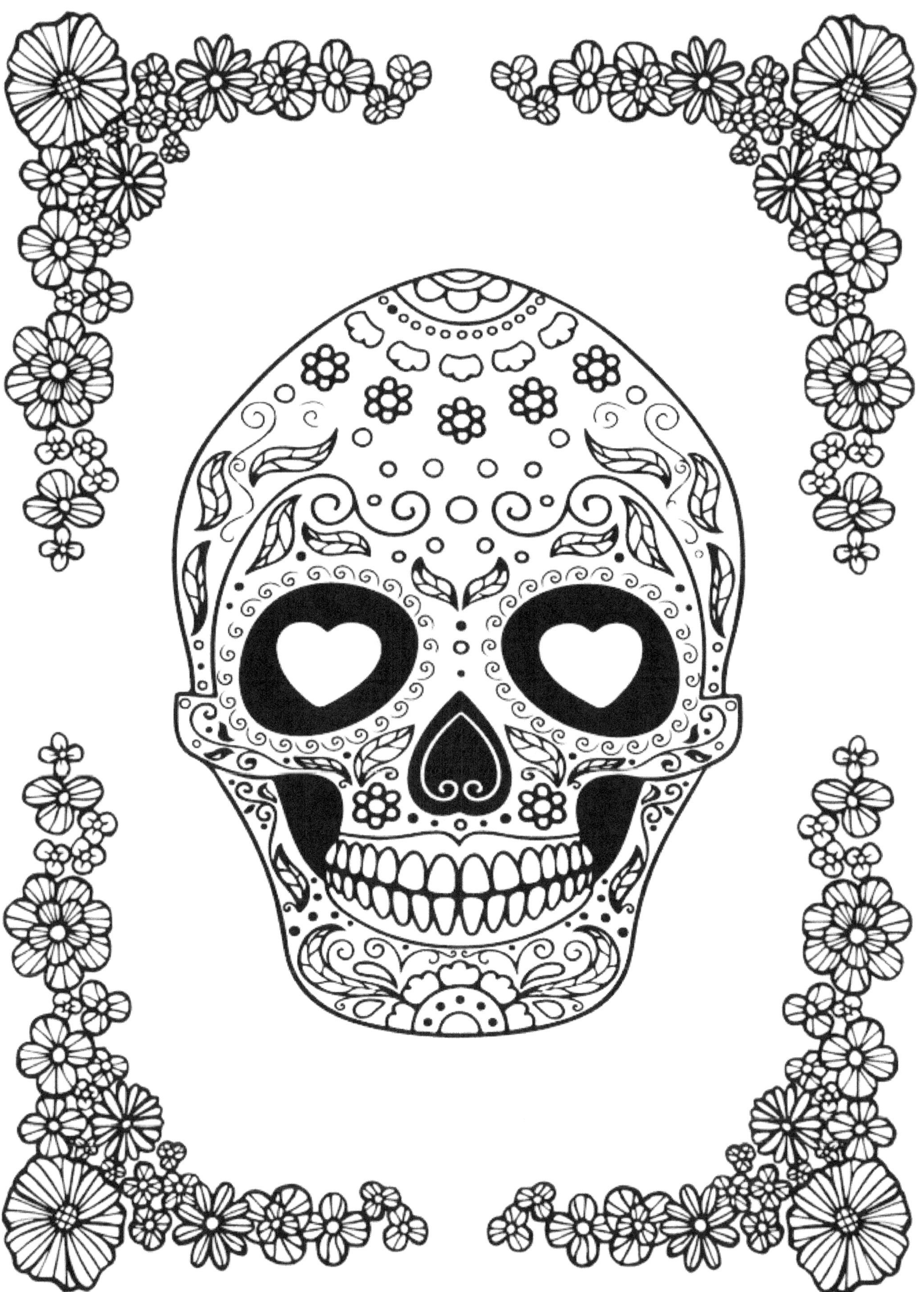

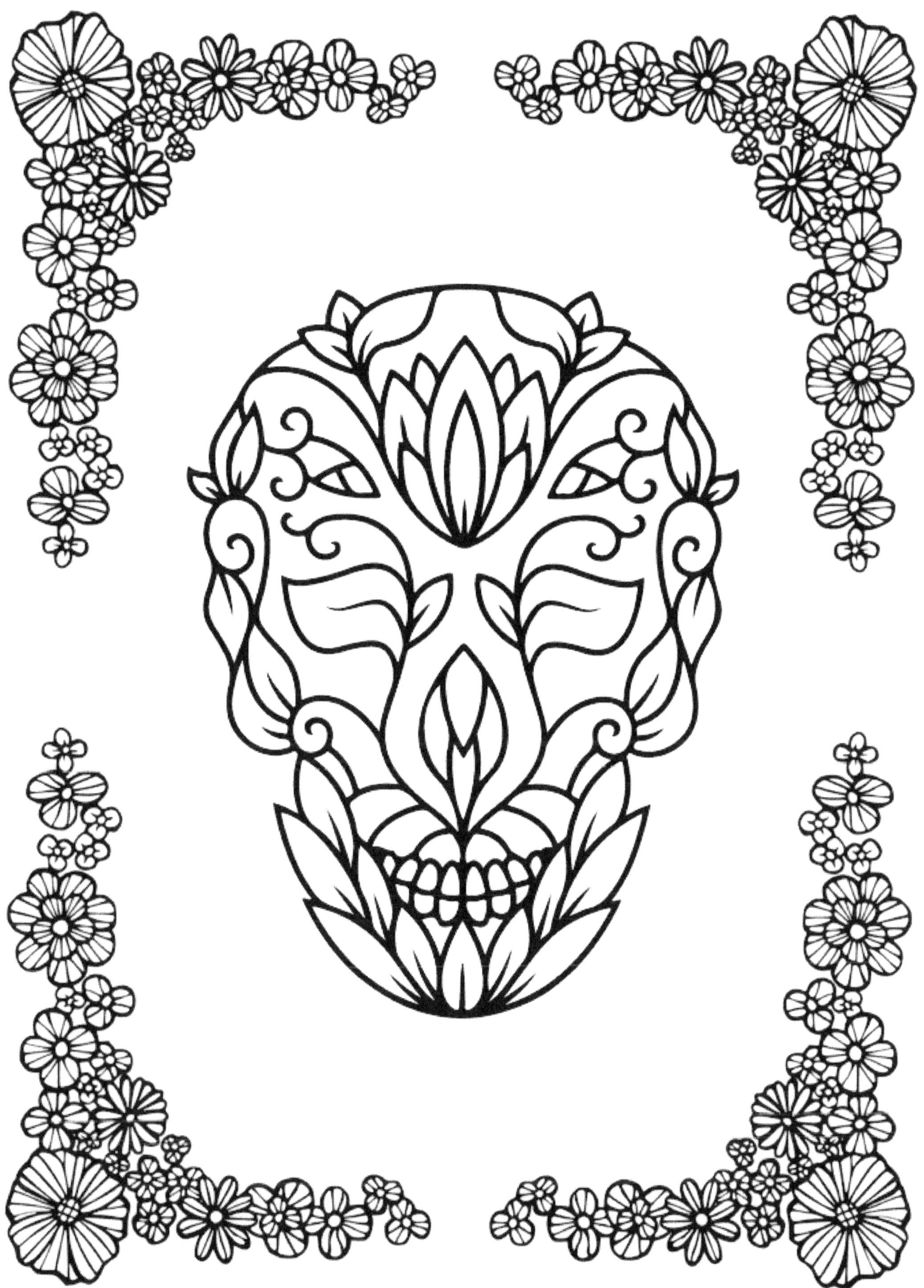

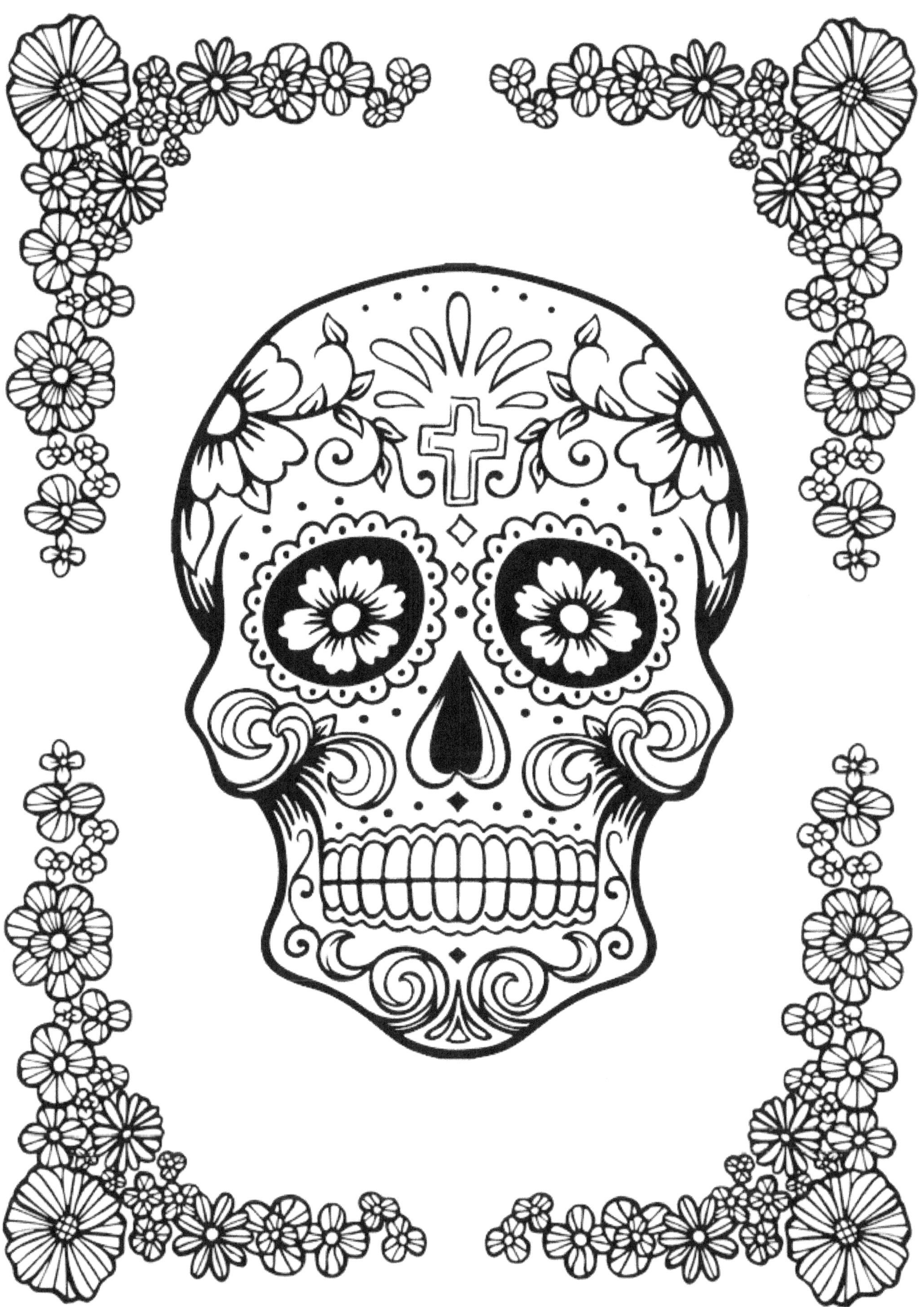

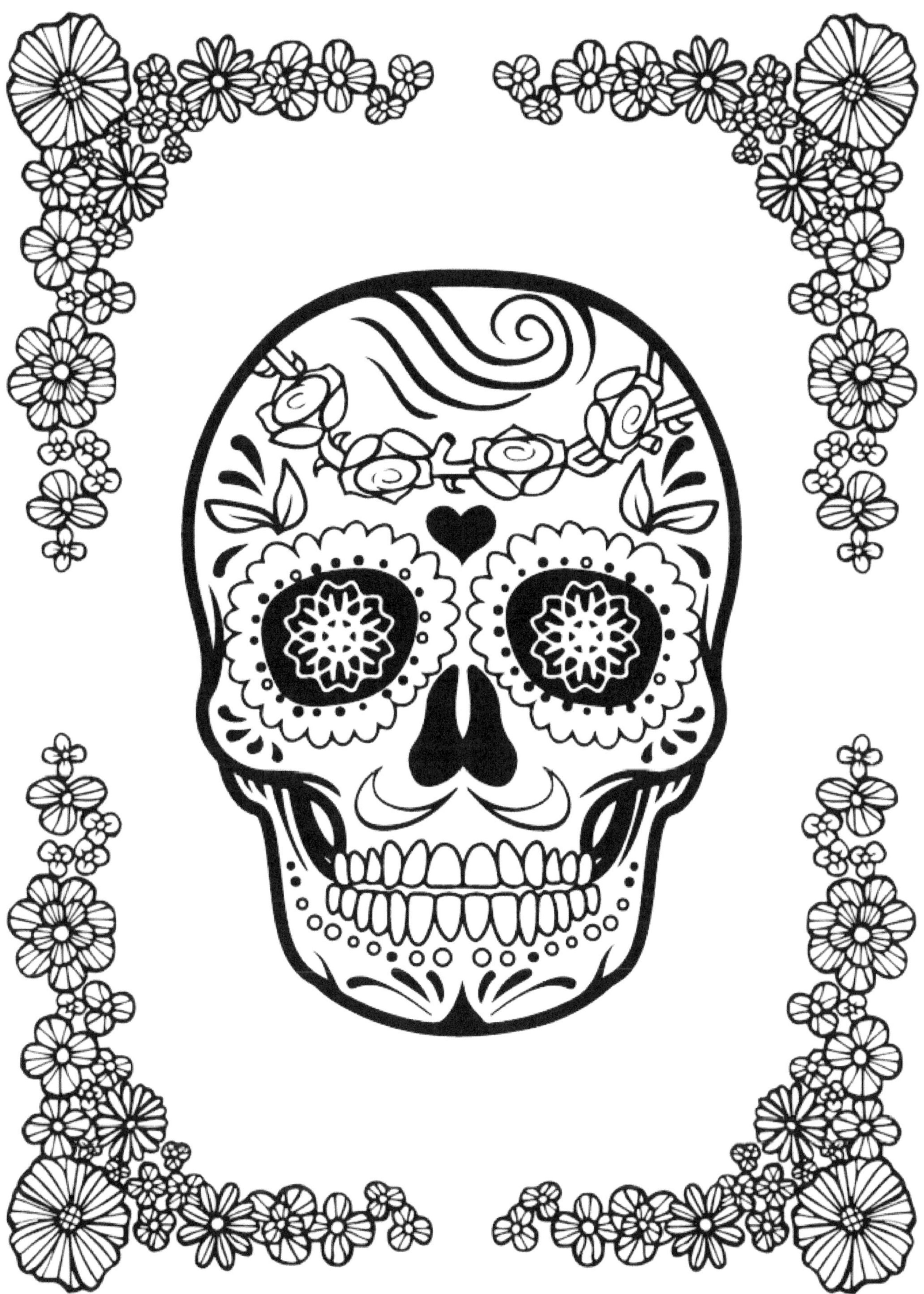

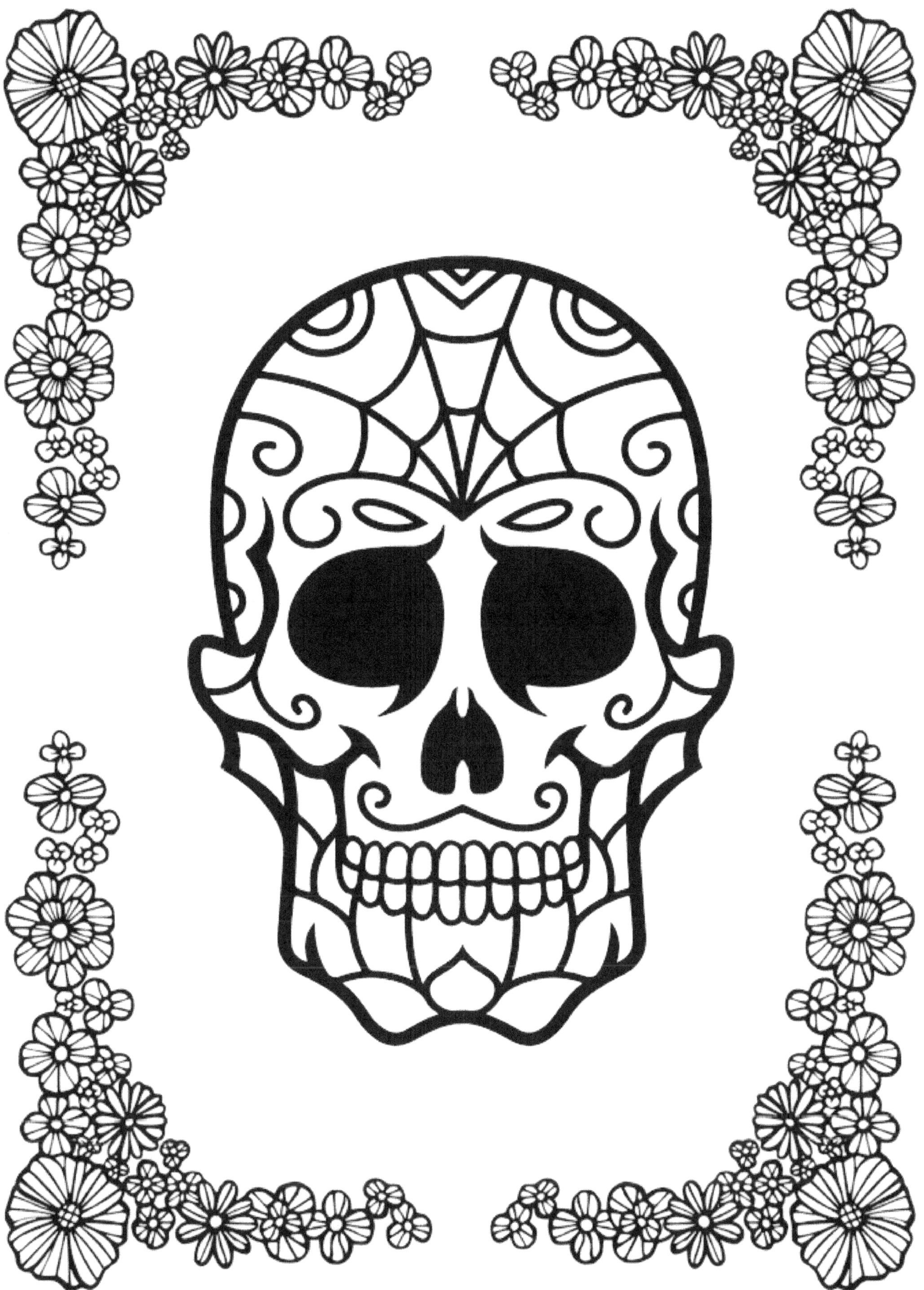

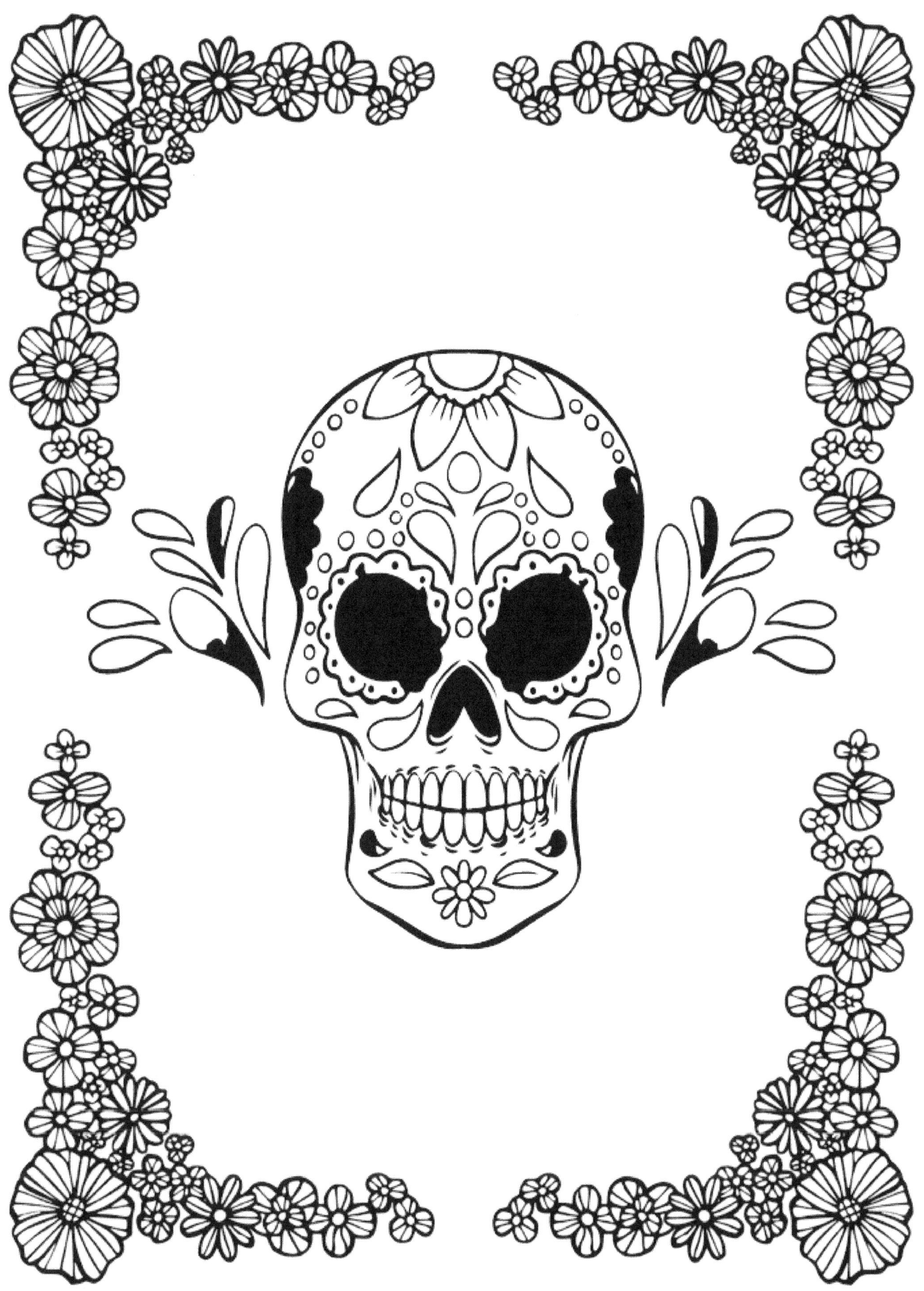

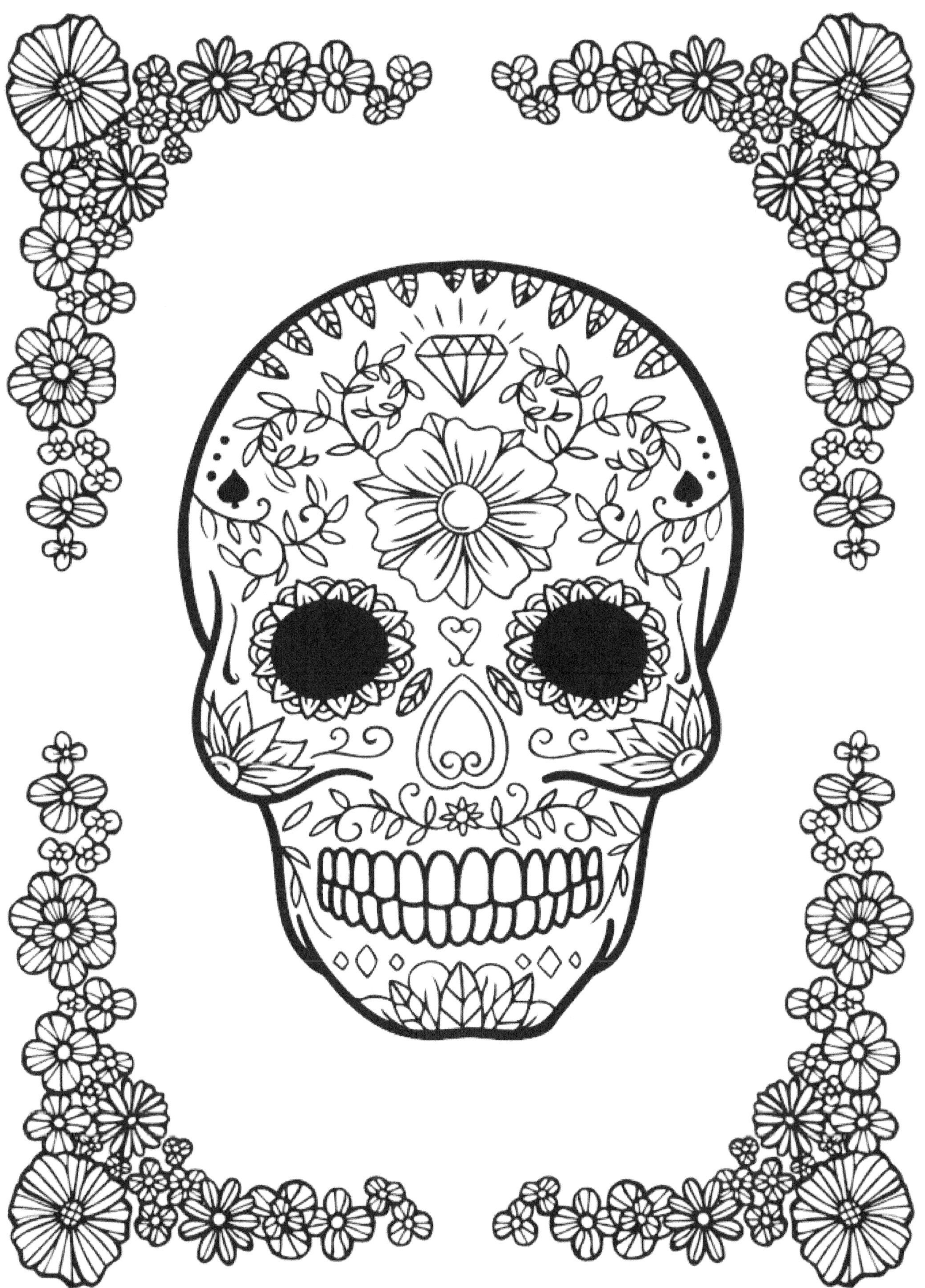

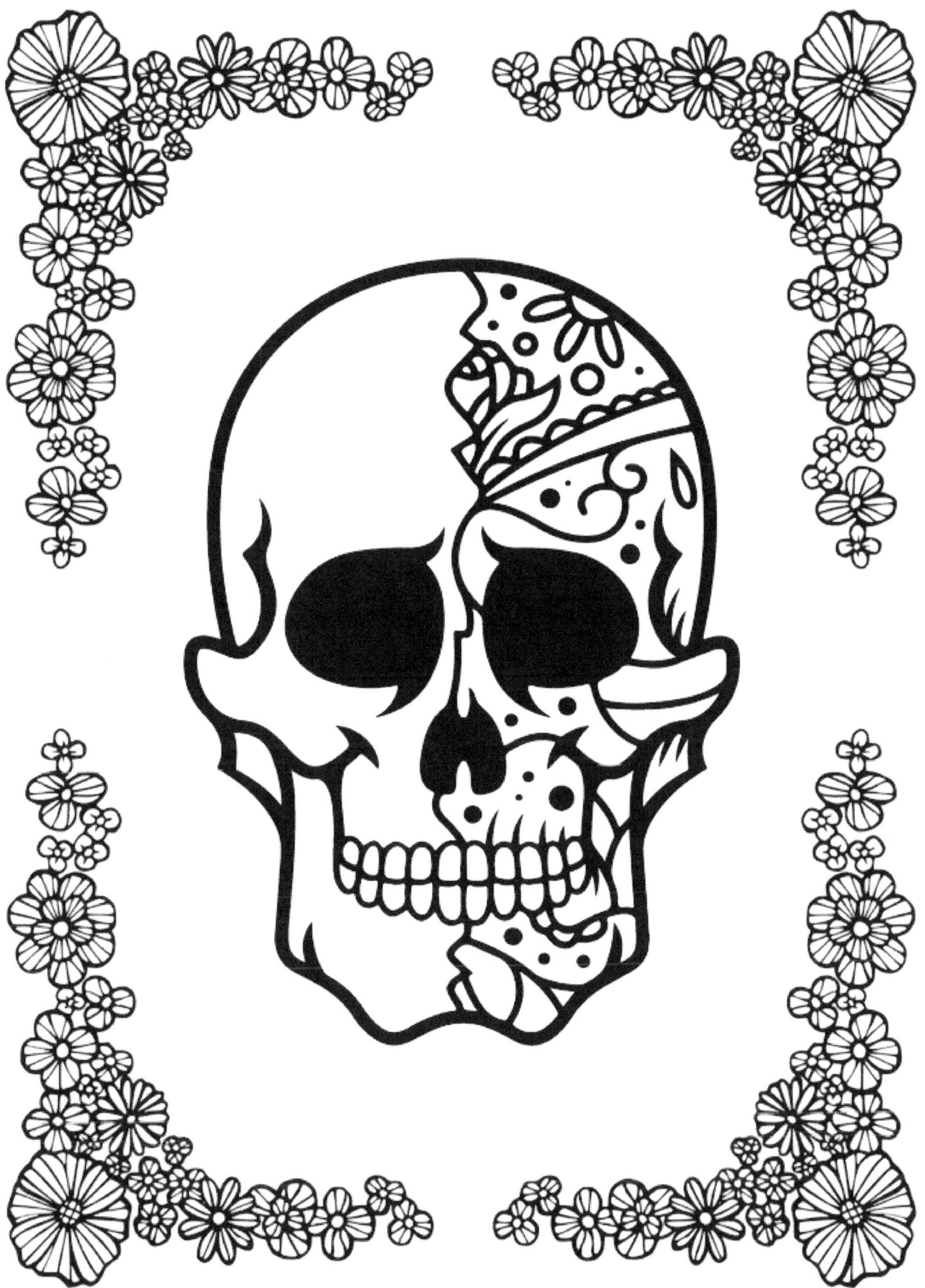

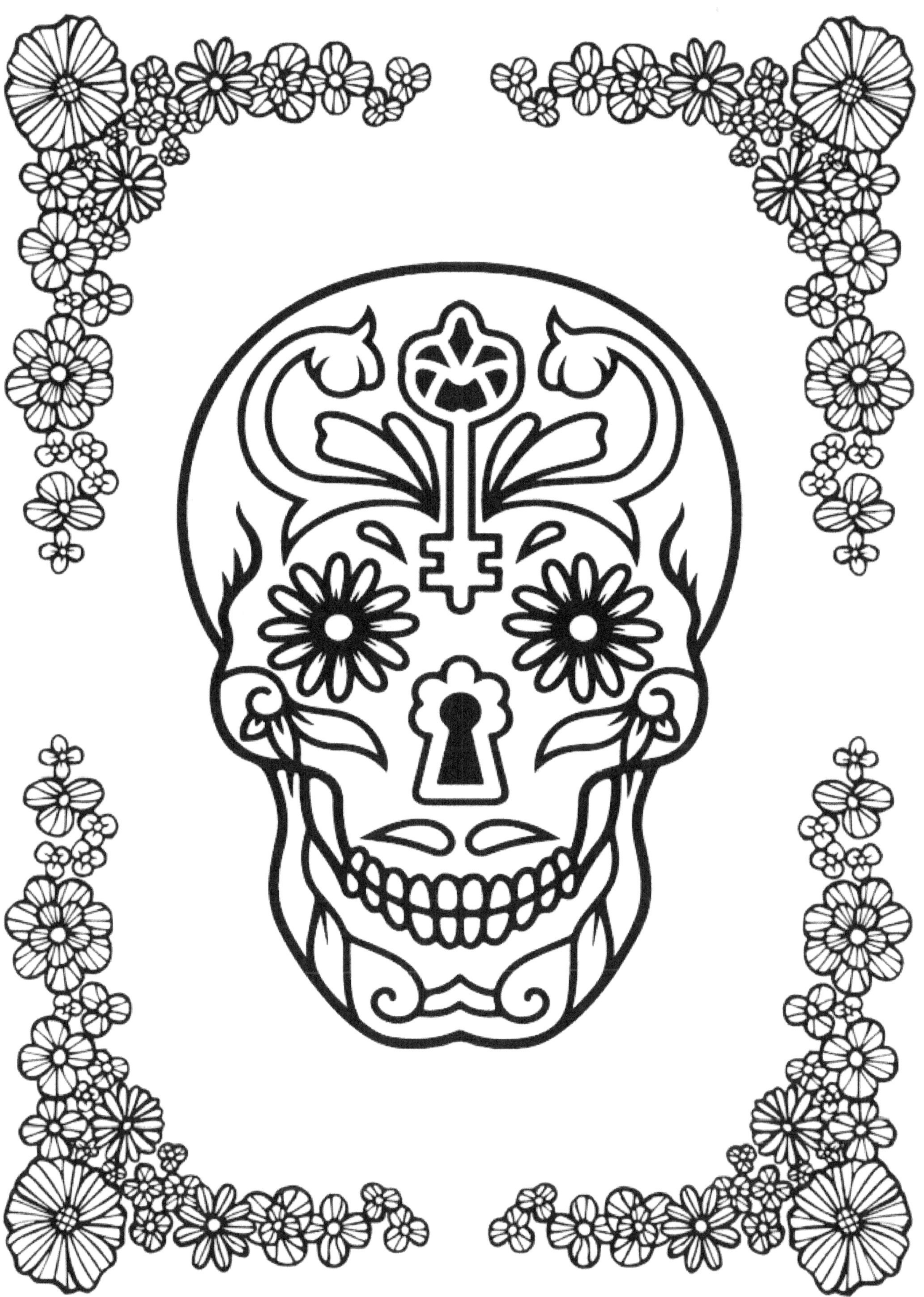

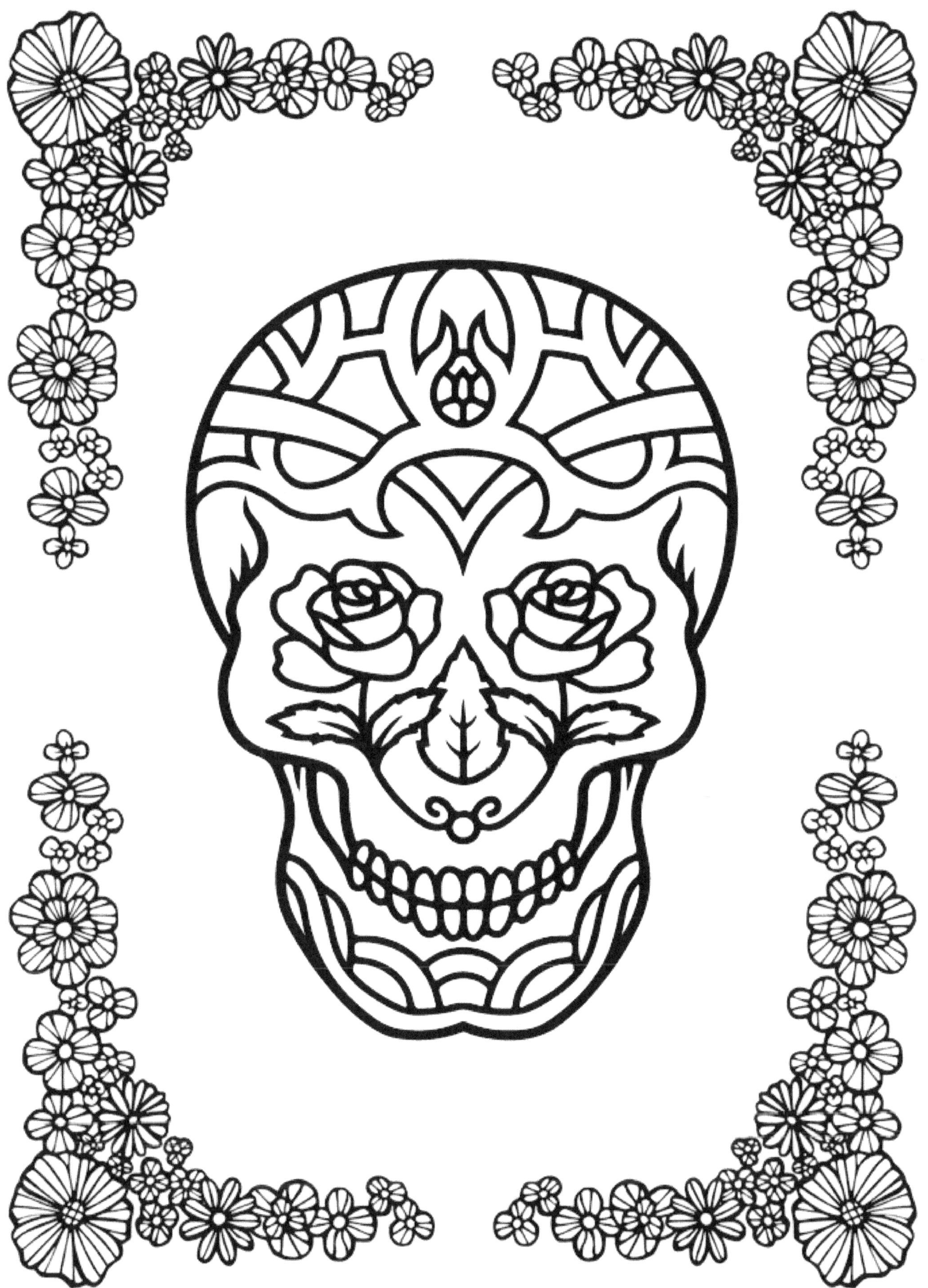

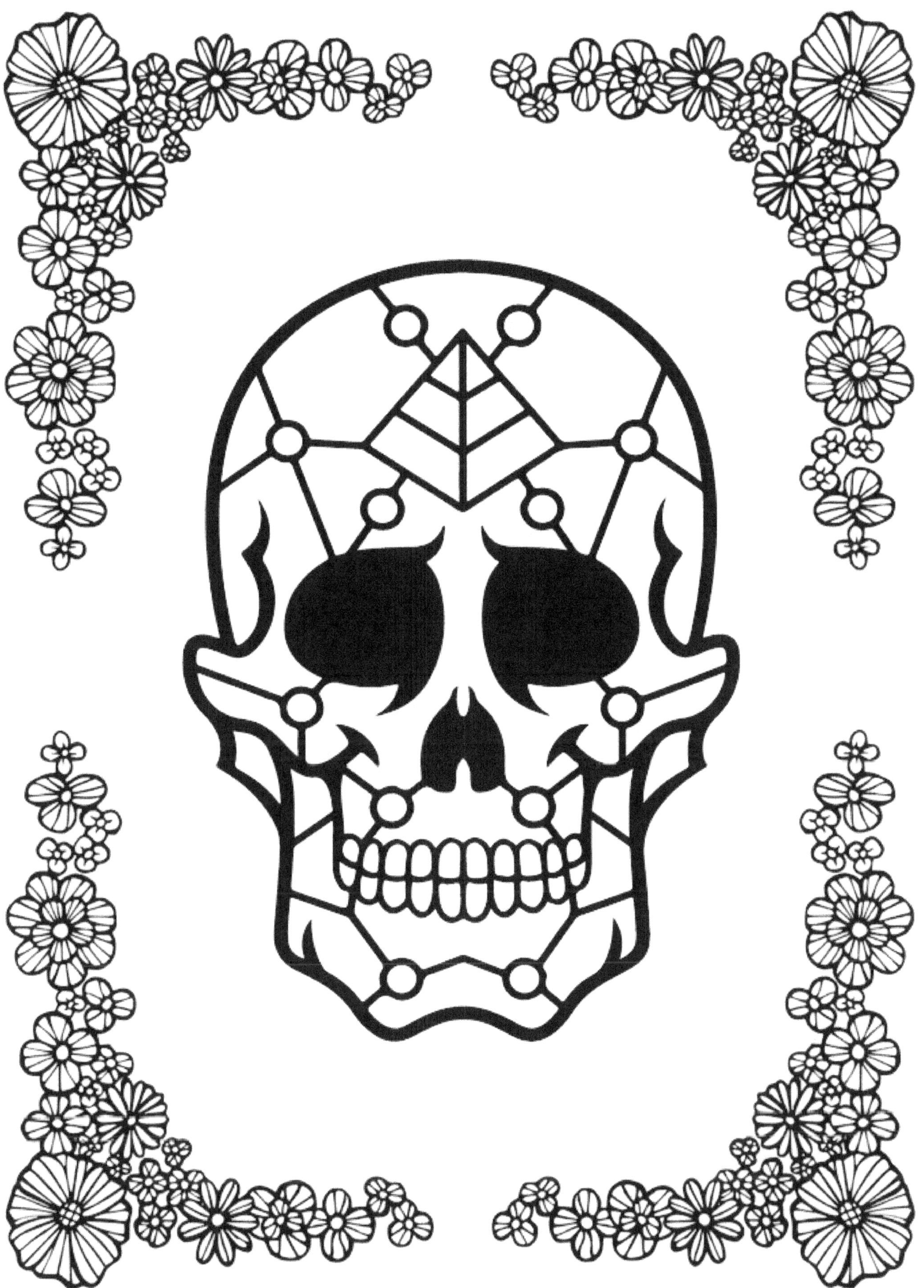

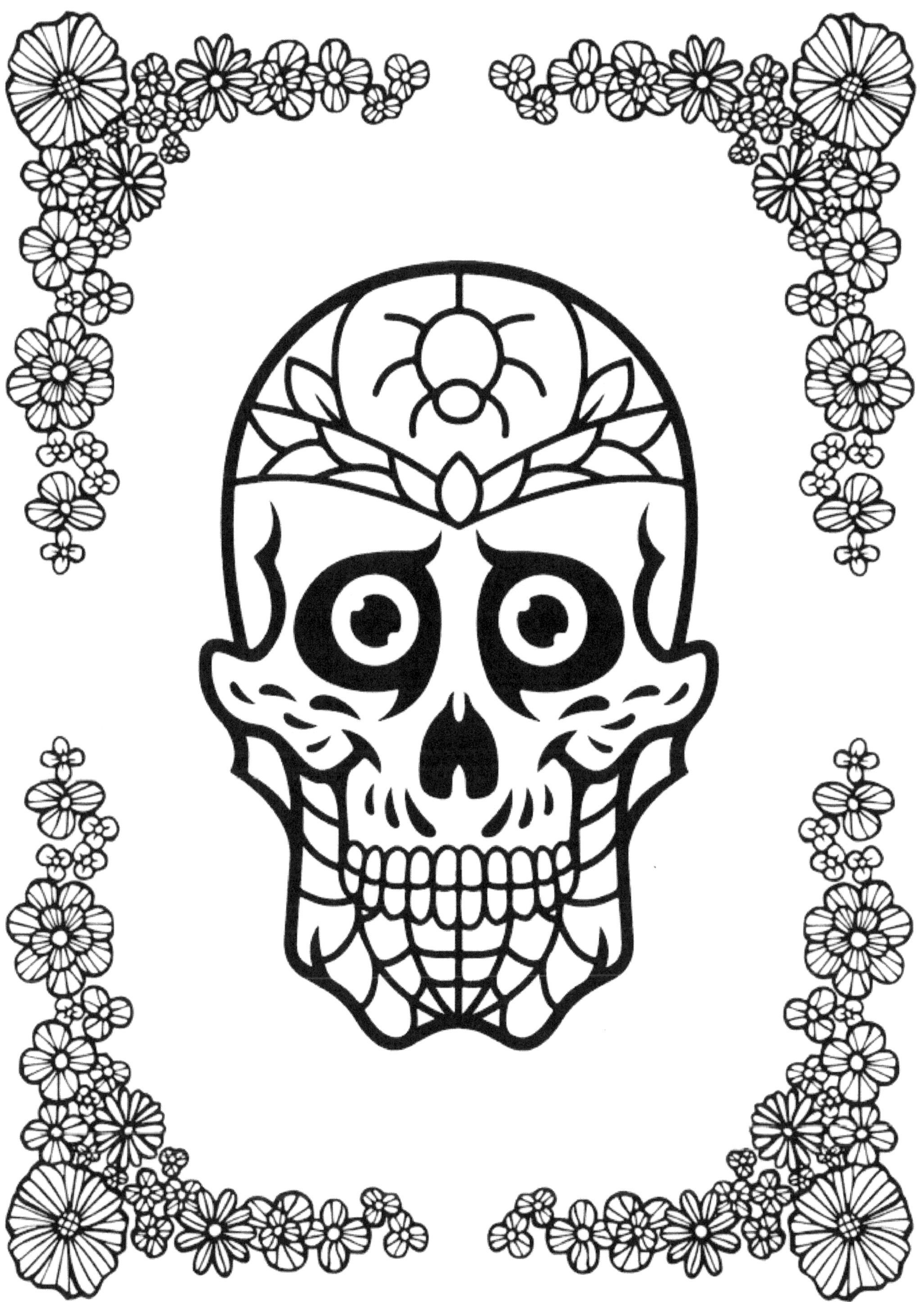

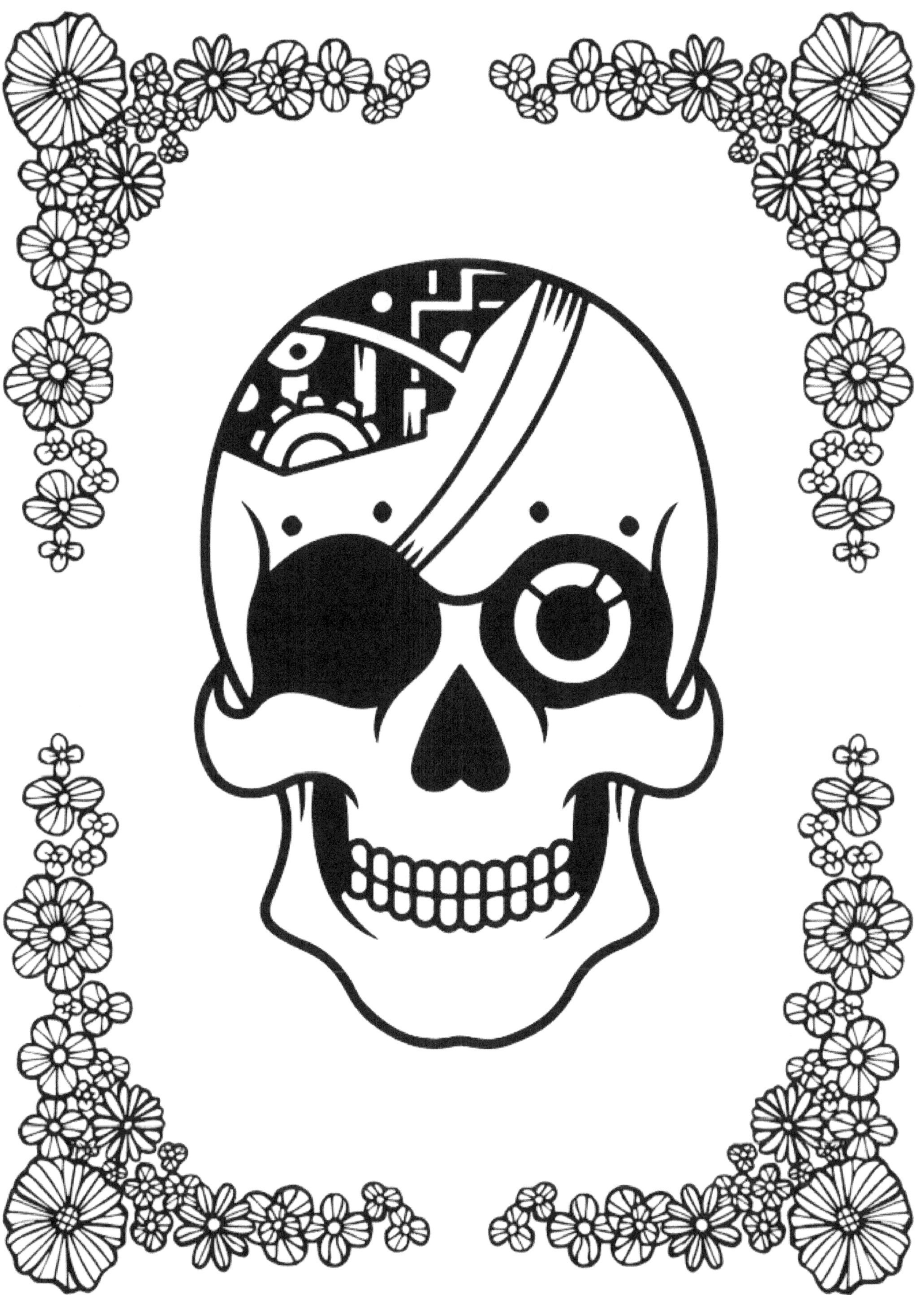

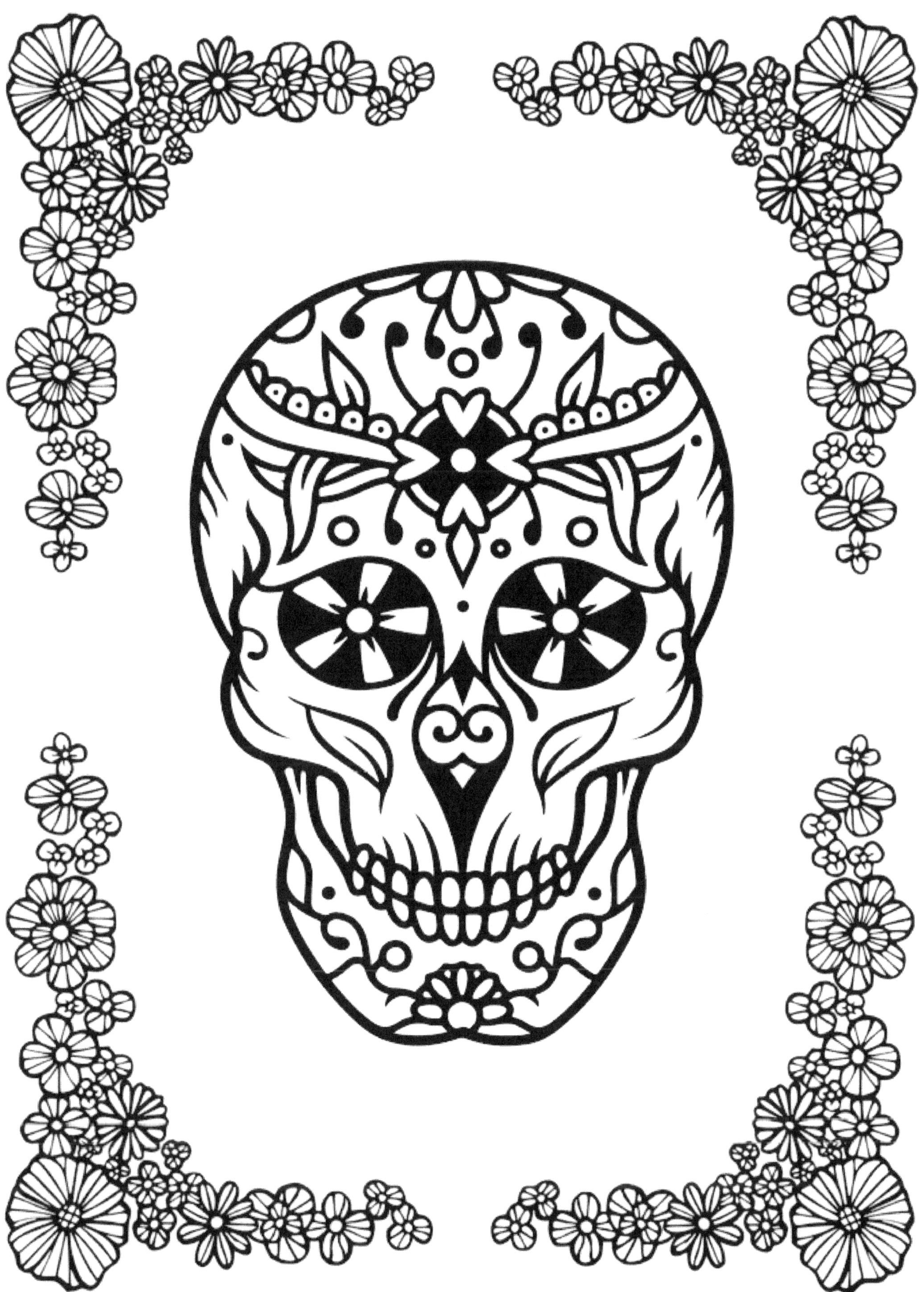

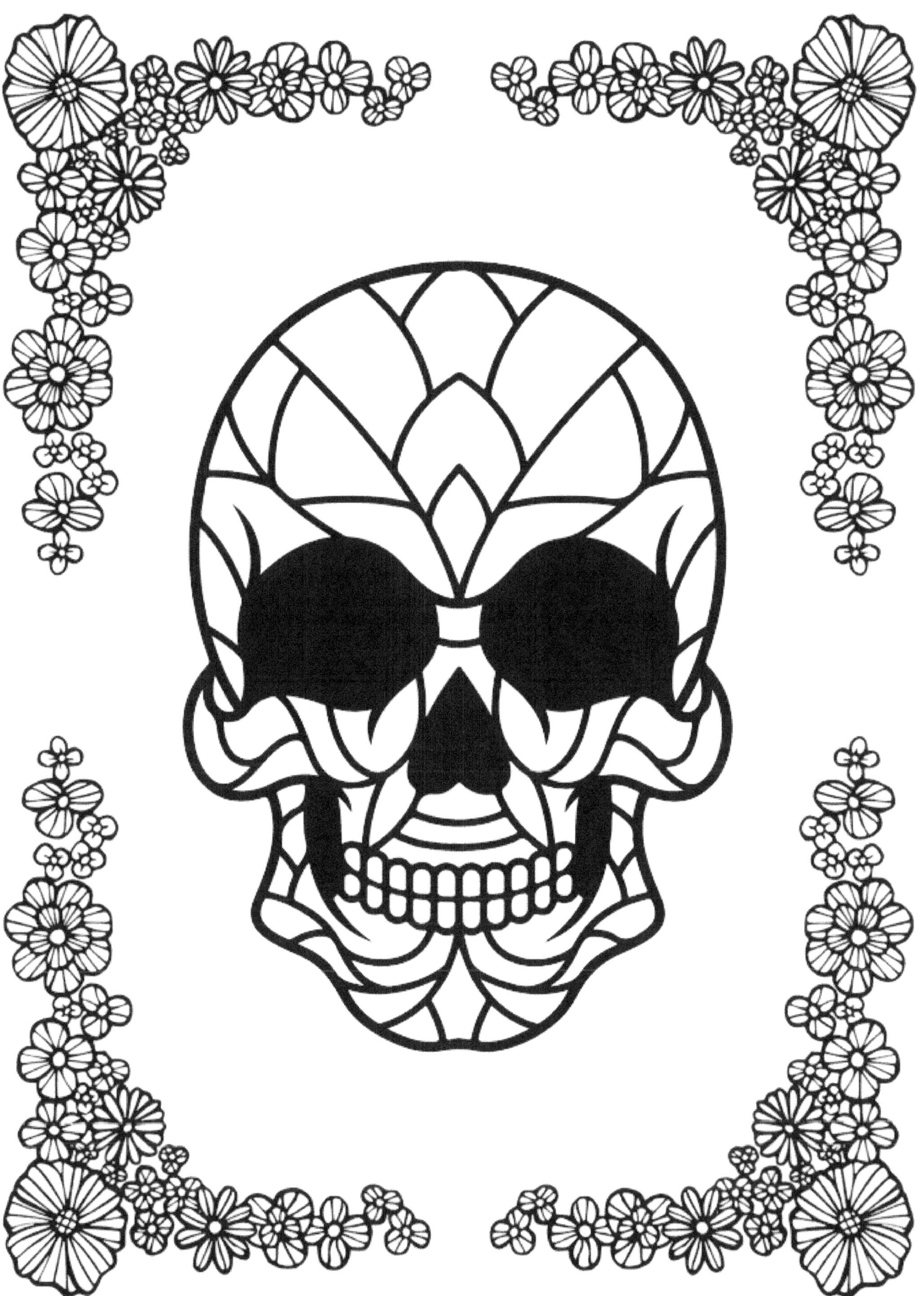

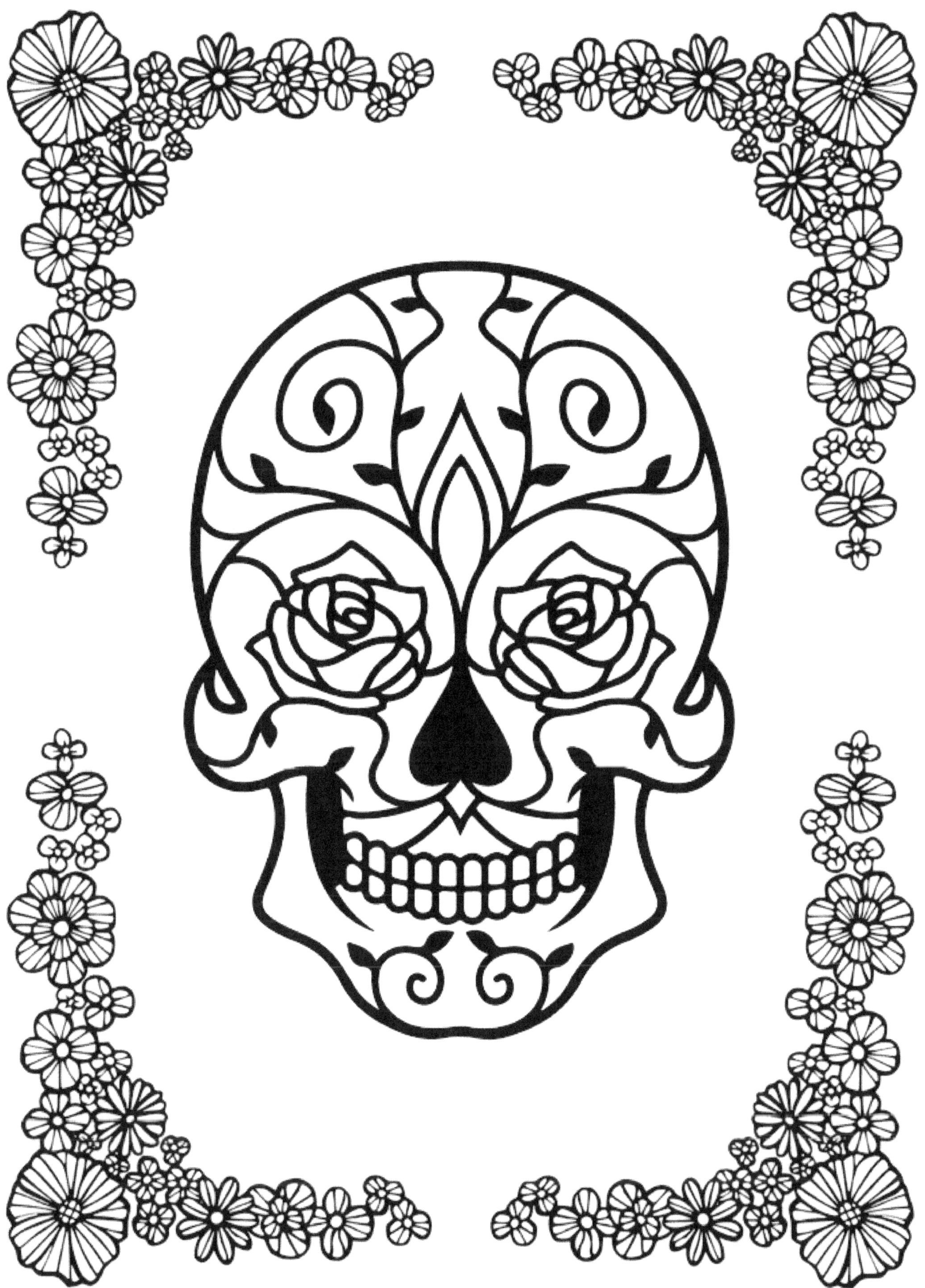

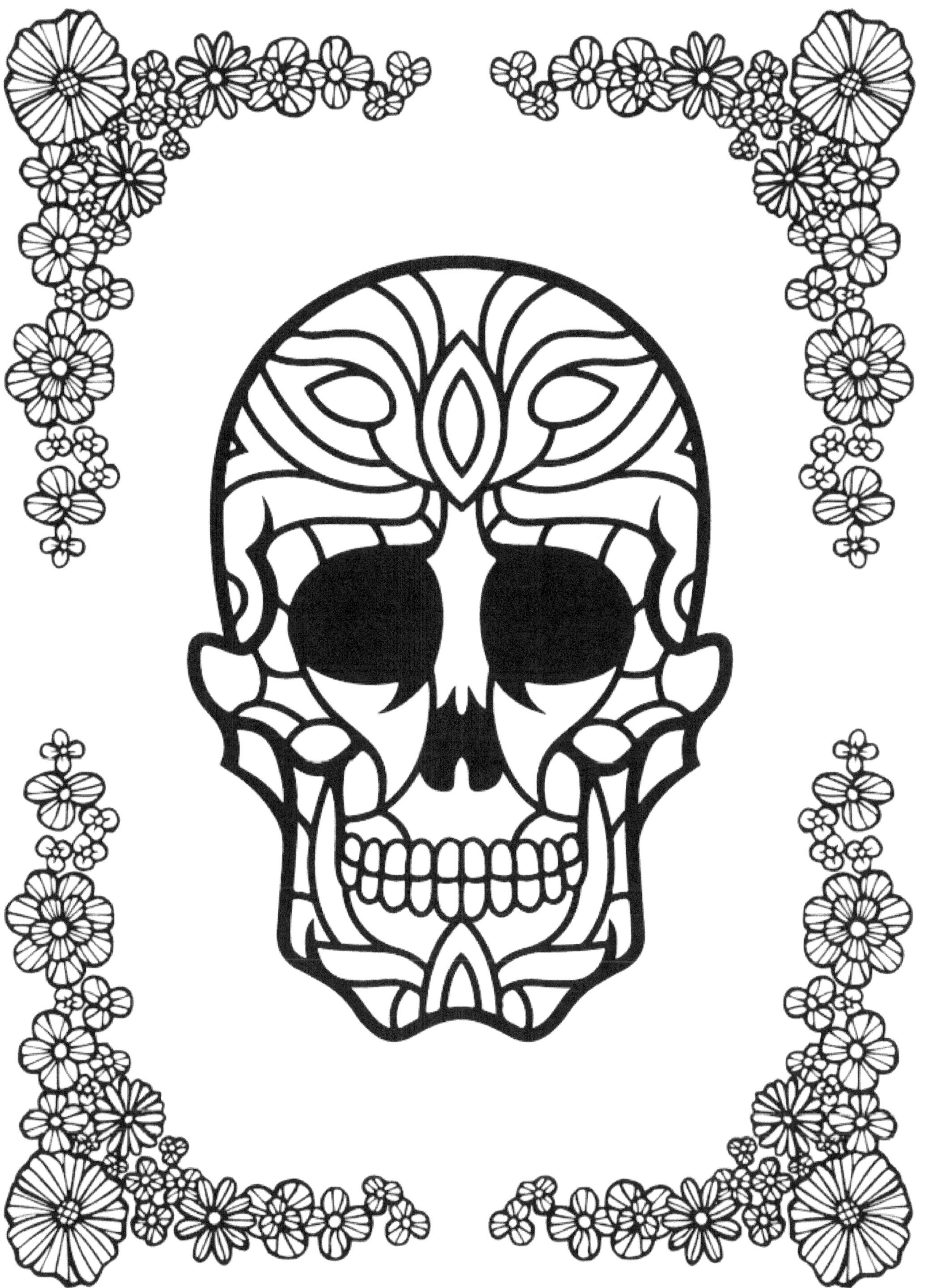

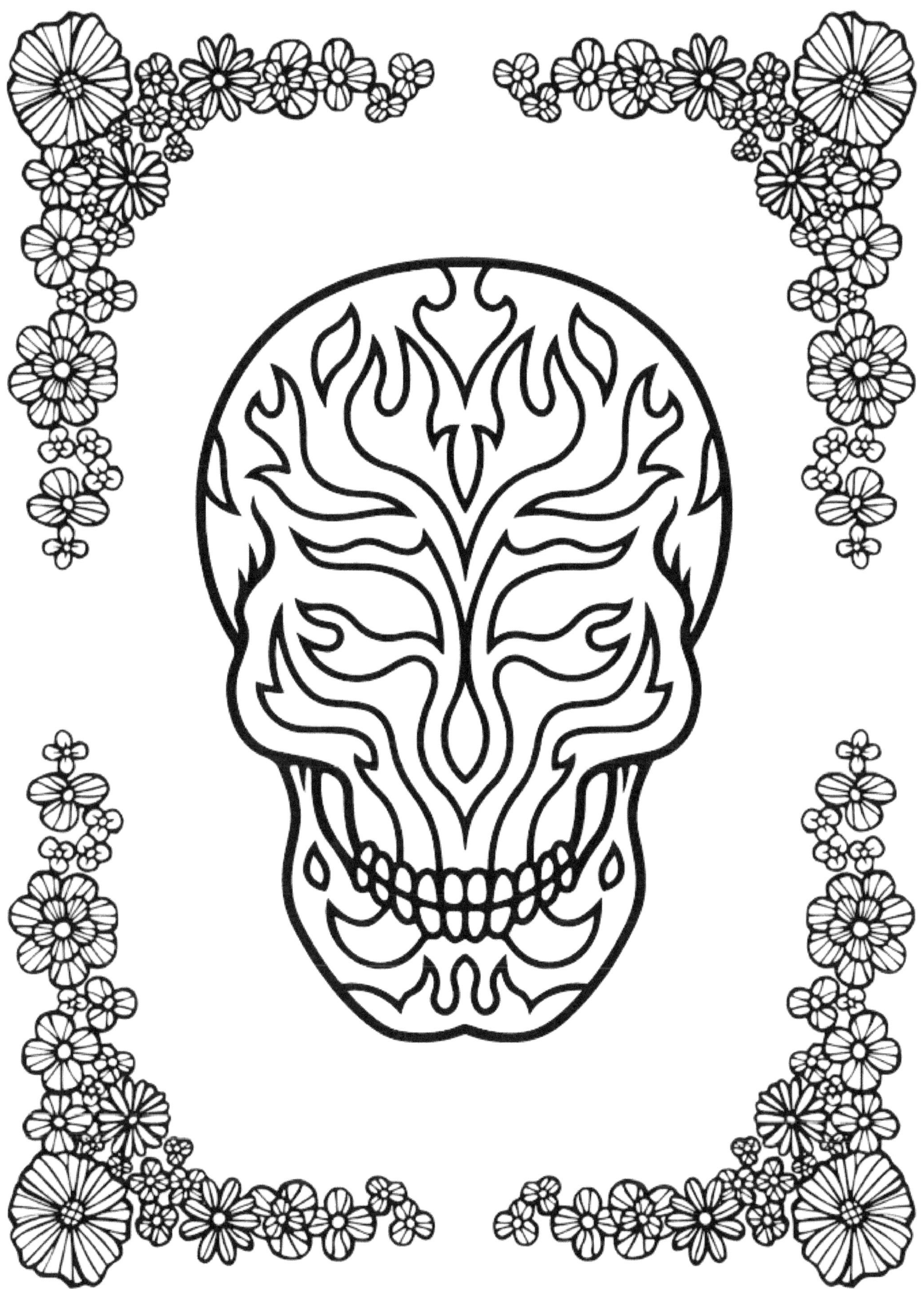

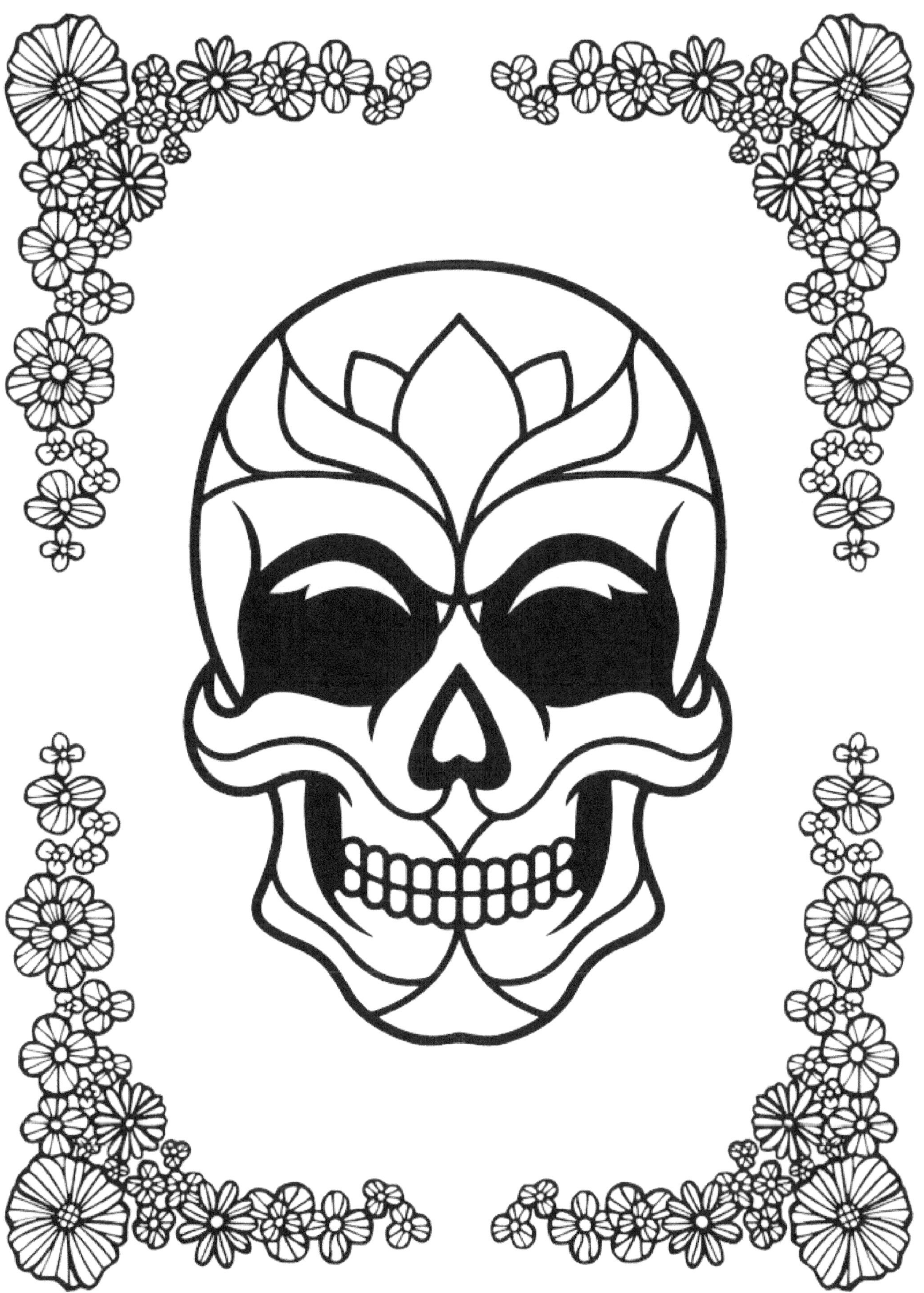

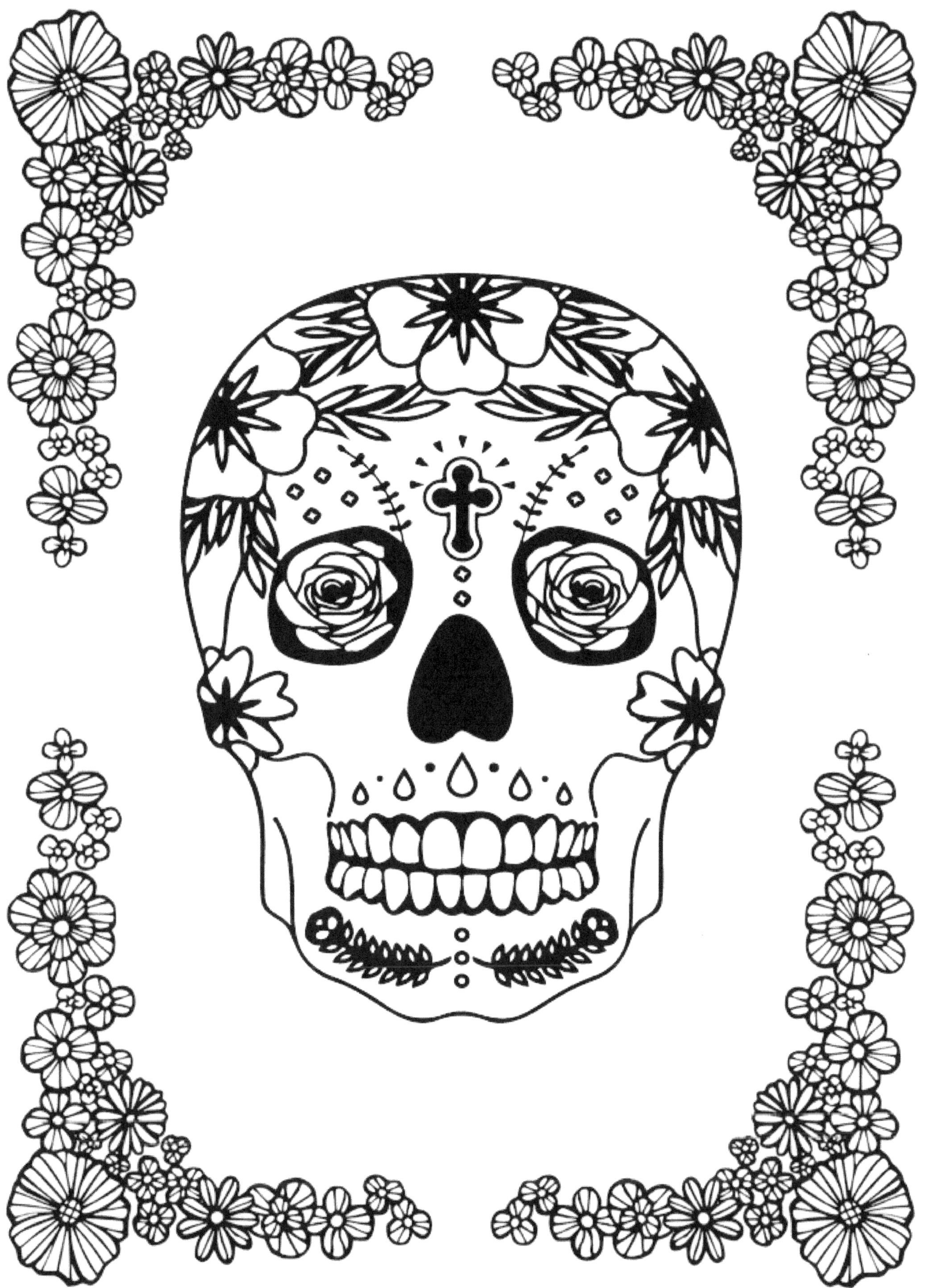

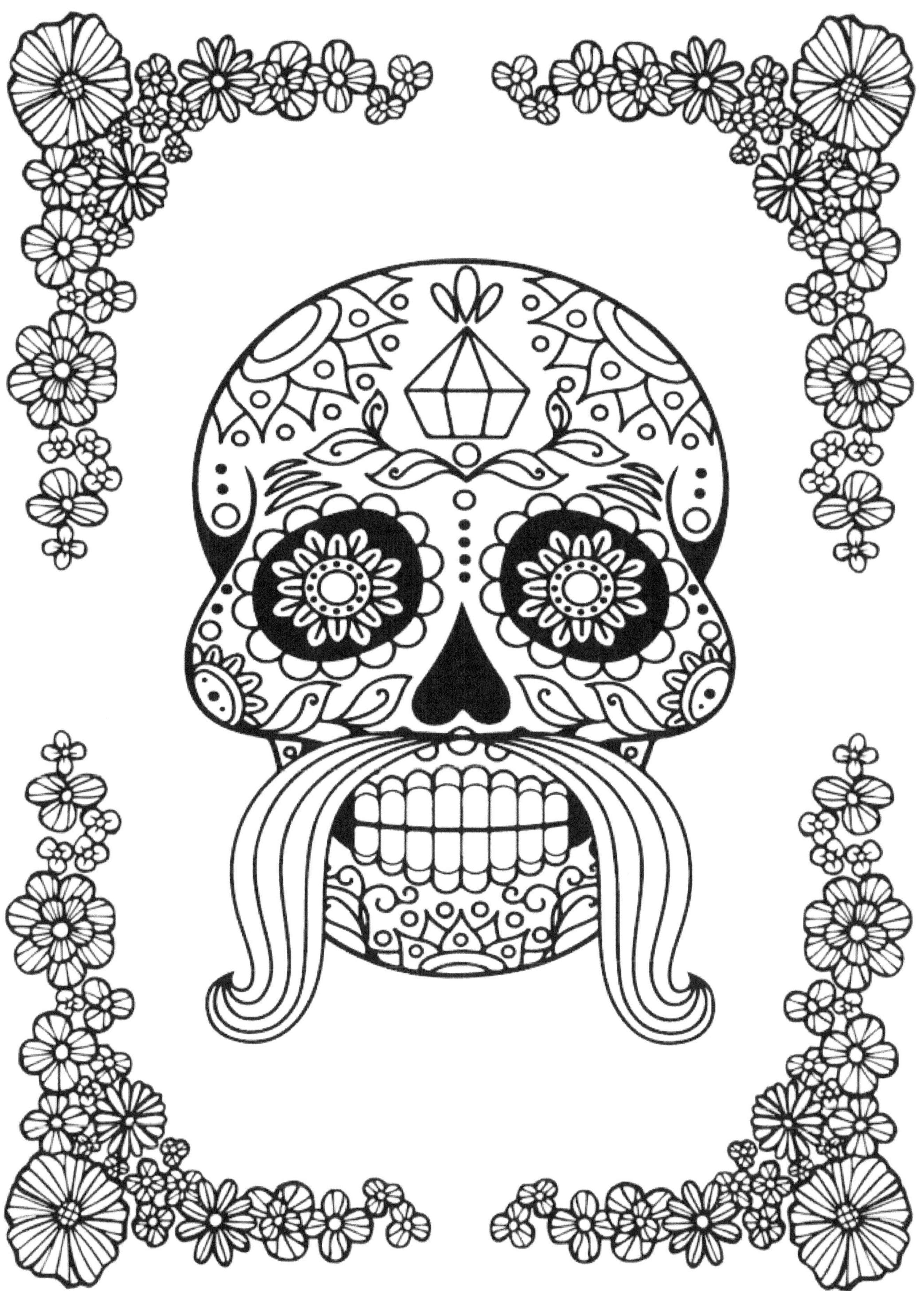